Idiomatic English

(How to Write and Speak It)

Published by :
Lotus Press Publishers & Distributors

Idiomatic English

(How to Write and Speak It)

Reena Gupta

4735/22, Prakash Deep Building
Ansari Road, Darya Ganj,
New Delhi - 110002

Lotus Press : Publishers & Distributors
Unit No. 220, 2nd Floor, 4735/22, Prakash Deep Building,
Ansari Road, Darya Ganj, New Delhi- 110002
Ph.: 98118-38000
• E-mail : lotuspress1984@gmail.com
www.lotuspress.co.in

Idiomatic English (How to Write and Speak It)

ISBN: 978-81-8382-315-9

Printed & Published by : **Lotus Press Publisher & Distributors,** New Delhi-02

PREFACE

A student wishes to have a reasonably good grasp of English. He should learn the basic forms of English and how to use them, particularly commonly used idioms and phrases. Therefore, this book is prepared to assist students of English in learning more commonly used idioms and phrases.

Most, if not all, languages have numerous idioms. Therefore to really understand what is spoken or written in a language and to really speak or write reasonably well in a language, it is important to understand the common or basic idioms in that language.

Idioms differ from figurative language in that figurative language creates pictures of other things in what is spoken or written. There are thousands of idioms in English, as might well be true of other languages.

Our book deals with the idioms and phrasal verbs. It tells their meanings and use in a sentence. The phrases given in this book are very useful in various fields. It would take time to master all these idioms. That is not necessary, because many of them are either used by only a segment of the population of native speakers or are used by native speakers in rare situations.

We have tried our best to make the subject of Idioms and phrases easy, so that any student can understand it. We believe that grasping knowledge or power of intelligence merely depend upon the age or education. So the students who have grasping power can easily grasp the book.

Author

Contents

1

Idiom

An idiom is a combination of words that has a meaning that is different from the meanings of the individual words themselves. It is a phrase which does not always follow the normal rules of meaning and grammar. It can have a literal meaning in one situation and a different idiomatic meaning in another situation.

Examples:

To sit on the fence can literally mean that one is sitting on a fence.

I sat on the fence and watched the game.

However, the idiomatic meaning of to sit on the fence is to not clearly choose a side regarding some issue.

The politician sat on the fence and would not clearly state his opinion about the tax issue.

Many English idioms are similar to expressions in other languages and can be easy for a learner to understand.

Other idioms come from older phrases which have changed over time.

Examples:

To hold one's horses means to stop and wait patiently for someone or something. It comes from a time when people rode horses and would have to hold their horses while waiting for someone or something.

"Hold your horses," the man said when his friend started to leave the store.

Other idioms come from such things as sports and may require some special cultural knowledge to understand them.

Examples:

To cover all of one's bases means to thoroughly prepare for or deal with a situation. It comes from the American game of baseball where you must cover or protect the bases.

I tried to cover all of my bases as I prepared for the job interview.

2

Structure of Idioms

1. Most idioms are fixed in their grammatical structure.

Examples:

- The expression to sit on the fence cannot become to sit on a fence or to sit on the fences.

2. Other idioms are the result of a change in grammatical structure and would generally be considered to be incorrect.

Examples:

- To be broken literally means that something is broken.
- The lamp is broken so I cannot read my book.
- To be broke is grammatically incorrect but it has the idiomatic meaning of to have no money.
- I am broke and I cannot go to a movie tonight.

3. There can also be changes in nouns, pronouns or in the verb tenses.

Examples:

- I sat on the fence and did not give my opinion.
- Many people are sitting on the fence and have not made a decision.

4. Adjectives and adverbs can also be added to an idiomatic phrase.

Examples:

- The politician has been sitting squarely in the middle of the fence since the election.
- That is why it is sometimes difficult to isolate the actual idiomatic expression and then find it in a dictionary of idioms.

3

Phrase and Its Types

A phrase is a group of related words (within a sentence) without both subject and verb.

Examples:

He is laughing at the joker.

A phrase functions as a noun, verb, adverb, adjective or preposition in a sentence. The function of a phrase depends on its construction (words it contains).

Types of Phrases

On the basis of their functions and constructions, phrases are divided into various types.

Noun Phrase

A noun phrase consists of a noun and other related words (usually modifiers and determiners) which modify the noun. It functions like a noun in a sentence.

A noun phrase consists of a noun as the head word and

other words (usually modifiers and determiners) which come after or before the noun. The whole phrase works as a noun in a sentence.

Noun Phrase = noun + modifiers (the modifiers can be after or before noun)

Examples:

- He is wearing a nice blue shirt. (as noun/object)
- He brought a glass full of milk. (as noun/object)
- The girl with black hair is laughing. (as noun/subject)
- A man on the roof was shouting. (as noun/subject)
- The girl with blue eyes bought a beautiful chair. (A sentence can also contain more noun phrases.)

Pre-positional Phrase

A pre-positional phrase consists of a preposition, objects of preposition (noun or pronoun) and may also consist of other modifiers. It starts with a pre-position and mostly ends with a noun or pronoun. Whatever pre-positional phrase ends with is called object of preposition. A pre-positional phrase functions as an adjective or adverb in a sentence.

Examples:

As adjective

- A man on the roof is singing a song.
- The lady in the room is our teacher.

As adverb

- He is shouting in a loud voice.

- She always behaves in a good manner.

Adjective Phrase

An adjective phrase is a group of words that functions like an adjective in a sentence. It consists of adjectives, modifier and any word that modifies a noun or pronoun. It functions like an adjective to modify (or tell about) a noun or a pronoun in a sentence.

Examples:

- He is wearing a nice green shirt. (modifies shirt)
- The girl with black hair is singing a song. (modifies girl)
- He gave me a glass full of water. (modifies glass)
- A boy from India won the race. (modifies boy)

Adverb Phrase

An adverb phrase is a group of words that functions as an adverb in a sentence. It consists of adverbs or other words (preposition, noun, verb, modifiers) that make a group with works like an adverb in a sentence.

Examples:

- He always behaves in a good manner. (modifies verb behave)
- They were shouting in a loud voice. (modifies verb shout)
- She always drives with care. (modifies verb drive)
- She sat in a corner of the room. (modifies verb sit)
- He returned in a short while. (modifies verb return)

Verb Phrase

A verb phrase is a combination of main verb and its auxiliaries (helping verbs) in a sentence.

Examples:

- He is eating a mango.
- She has finished her work.
- You should study for the exam.
- She has been sleeping for three hours.

According to generative grammar, a verb phrase can consist of main verb, its auxiliaries, its complements and other modifiers. Hence, it can refer to the whole predicate of a sentence.

Infinitive Phrase

An infinitive phrase consist of an infinitive (to + simple form of verb) and modifiers or other words associated to the infinitive. An infinitive phrase always functions as an adjective, adverb or a noun in a sentence.

Examples:

- He likes to read books. (As noun/object)
- To earn money is a desire of everyone. (As noun/ subject)
- He shouted to inform people about the fire. (As adverb, modifies verb shout)
- He made a plan to buy a new bicycle. (As adjective, modifies noun plan)

Gerund Phrase

A gerund phrase consists of a gerund (verb + ing) and modifiers or other words associated with the gerund. A gerund phrase acts as a noun in a sentence.

Examples:

- I like writing good essays. (As noun/object)
- She started thinking about the problem. (As noun/object)
- Sleeping late in night is not a good habit. (As noun/subject)
- Weeping of a baby woke him up. (As noun/subject)

Participle Phrase

A participle phrase consists of a present participle (verb + ing), a past participle (verb ending in -ed or other form in case of irregular verbs) and modifiers or other associate words. A participle phrase is separated by commas. It always acts as an adjective in a sentence.

Examples:

- The kids, making a noise, need food. (modifies kids)
- I received a letter, mentioning about my exam. (modifies letter)
- The table, made of steel, is too expensive. (modifies table)
- We saw a car, damaged in an accident. (modifies car)

Absolute Phrase

Absolute phrase (also called nominative phrase) is a group of words including a noun or pronoun and a participle as well as any associated modifiers. Absolute phrase modifies (give information about) the entire sentence. It resembles a clause but it lack a true finite verb. It is separated by a comma or pairs of commas from the rest sentence.

Examples:

- He looks sad, his face is expressing worry.
- She was waiting for her friend, her eyes on the clock.

Phrasal Verb

A phrasal verb is a two-part or three-part verb and is sometimes called a compound verb. It is a combination of a verb and an adverb, a verb and a preposition, and a verb with an adverb and a preposition.

It can have a literal meaning that is easy to understand because the meaning is clear from the words that are used. It can also have an idiomatic meaning which cannot easily be understood by looking at the words themselves.

Verb and Adverb (run + around)

1. to run around (something) - to run in a circle around something (literal meaning)

Example:

- The dog ran around the well.

2. to run around (somewhere) - to go to various places to do something (idiomatic meaning)

Example:

- I spent the day running around downtown.

Verb and Preposition (run + into)

1. to run into (someone or something) - to hit or crash into someone or something (literal meaning)

Example:

- The car ran into the truck on the busy street.

2. to run into (someone) - to meet someone by chance (idiomatic meaning)

Example:

- I ran into my friend in a restaurant yesterday.

Verb and Adverb and Preposition (run + around + with)

1. to run around with (someone) - to be friends and do things with someone or with a group of people (idiomatic meaning)

Example:

- The boy is running around with a bad group of people.

2. to run (verb) around (adverb) like a chicken with its head cut off - to run around with no purpose

Example:

- I ran around like a chicken with its head cut off as I prepared for my holidays.

4

Some Grammatical Terms

Adjective (adj.)

An adjective is word used to describe a noun (*e.g.*, good, bad, enjoyable, tedious.)

Adverb (adv.)

An adverb is a word that describes how the verb is performed (*e.g.*, quickly, slowly, carefully).

Clause

A clause is a minimal group of words that makes sense in English. A clause often, though not always, contains a subject. It will generally contain a verb, and often it contains an object or another structure as well. A clause can be independent (this is known as a 'main clause') or dependent on the other part of the sentence (known as a 'sub-ordinate caluse').

Countable Noun (N. Count)

A countable noun is a noun that can be counted in terms of number (*e.g.*, a table, a chair).

Definite Article

The definite article ('the') is used together with a noun when the reference is specific.

Gerund

This is the 'ing' form of the verb that is used after certain prepositions (*e.g.*, by) and after certain verbs (*e.g.*, to enjoy).

Indefinite Article

The indefinite article ('a', 'an') is used together with a noun when the reference is not specific. 'A' or 'An' cannot be used before an uncountable noun.

Infinitive (inf.)

This is the basic form of the verb that has not been changed to indicate the person (*e.g.*, (to) play, to enjoy).

Intransitive Verb (v.i.)

This is a verb that has no object after it (*e.g.*, to die).

Modal Verb

A modal verb is a special kind of verb (known as an auxiliary verb) which describes the way a speaker feels about a situation (*e.g.*, whether the speaker thinks that the situation is possible or impossible, advisable or inadvisable). Common examples are 'can', 'could', 'may', 'might'. 'must', 'have to', 'should', 'will', 'would', etc.

Noun (n.)

A noun is the name of a person, place, thing or abstract quality (*e.g.*, kindness).

Object (o.)

An object is a person or thing that 'receives' the action.

Passive Voice

This is a type of sentence where the focus is on the object that 'receives' the action, and the action itself (not the subject, as is usually the case).

Phrasal Verb

This is a verb that contains one or two particles after it (*e.g.*, to get on with, to put up with, etc). The meaning is often idiomatic.

Preposition

This is a small word which is used with place (*e.g.*, 'at home'), time (*e.g.*, 'in the afternoon'), after certain verbs (*e.g.*, it depends on) and with particular expressions (*e.g.*, let's get down to business)

Relative Word

This a word like 'who', 'whom', 'which' and 'whose' which indicates relationships and belonging.

Sentence

A sentence is a group of words with at least one main (independent) clause. The shortest sentence must contain at least a subject and verb (*e.g.*, 'He arrived').

Subject

A subject is a person or thing that 'does' the action.

Tense

Tenses are used to refer to different time frames (past, present and future). There is no simple relationship between tense and time in English.

Transitive Verb (v.t)

This is a verb that is followed by an object (*e.g.*, to watch).

Uncountable Noun (N. Uncount.)

An uncountable noun is a noun that cannot be counted in terms of number (*e.g.*, water, oil).

Verb (v.)

A verb generally indicates an action (*e.g.*, play, happen) but can also refer to mental processes (*e.g.*, 'think', 'consider', 'imagine') and verbal processes (*e.g.*, 'write', 'conclude', 'emphasise').

5

'A-Z' Idioms

A big if

"A big if" is used when a person wants to emphasize the word if. It is typically used at the end of the phrase.

Example:

- If we decide to go to New York, we will go to the theater.

Above board

If the company or a person is doing thing illegally, then they are not "above board." Essentially, it means, is the company genuine?

Example:

- I have no way of knowing if this company is above board or not.

Above and beyond the call of duty

It means that someone has done much more than was required of him. It is obviously a compliment.

Example:

- I gave him the afternoon off because he went above and beyond the call of duty yesterday.

Acid test

"Acid tests" occur often outside of the laboratory, which is where the term originated. Simply, they are standards that we use to determine whether something (or someone) is good or not. An acid test is simply a test.

Example:

- It was an acid test to see if I knew what I was talking about regarding the writing process.

A cinch

This is a word that means something that is very very easy to do.

Example:

- It is a cinch to dial on a telephone.

Ahead of his time

If someone is "ahead of his time," it means that he is forward-thinking and innovative.

Example:

- Even now we consider Einstein to be ahead of his time.

A hop skip and jump away

Something that is a "hop skip and jump away" is a place that is very close.

Example:

- He lives only a hop skip and jump away from my house.

All in all

It means overall or generally.

Example:

- All in all, the meeting went better than expected.

All squared away

Everything is in order is the best definition for "all squared away."

Example:

- The phone bill is all squared away, mom.

All talk and no action

It means that a person boasts about being able to do something but does not follow through by actually doing it.

Example:

- Don't listen to Simmi. She's all talk and no action when it comes to making decisions.

All thumbs

It means that a person has a difficulty in doing simple mechanical tasks.

Example:

- When it comes to building things, Rahul was all thumbs.

And then there was light

Typically, this phrase is spoken when a group of people are physically in the dark and the light suddenly appears (or is turned on).

Example:

- We were just waiting for her and then there was light.

An old hat at that

If you are "an old hat" you do something well. You do it effortlessly.

Example:

- Kamal is an old hat with cameras.

Another trick up your sleeve

This idiom means that a person has other options if the one he is trying doesn't work. He is resourceful.

Example:

- I wouldn't worry about him. He always has another trick up his sleeve.

Antsy

A person who is "antsy" cannot sit still. He moves around in his seat and can't get comfortable. Children are often like this.

Example:

- Diksha was antsy all through the journey.

Argue until blue in the face

The meaning of this idiom is that a person argues and argues and argues but did not persuade you to change your mind.

Example:

- I argued with him until I was blue in the face.

A short fuse

If you have "a short fuse," you get angry quickly. It does not take much to anger you.

Example:

- Be careful around Mr. Thakur, he's got a short fuse.

A star is born

The phrase "a star is born" is used when a new performer makes it big.

Example:

- "Wow. A star is born." It is a great compliment.

A stone's throw away

A stone's throw away means very close, as in "if I threw a stone I could hit it." That's how close he lives.

Example:

- Sahil's house is only a stone's throw away from me.

At loggerheads with

This phrase simply means to be at odds with or quarreling.

Example:

- He was at loggerheads with the committee over funding.

At the drop of a hat

Simply, this phrase means instantly, immediately, or on demand. It implies that if someone wants me to do something specifically, I will drop what I am doing to do it.

Example:

- He would go out for a steak at the drop of a hat.

A yellow streak down your back

Typically, when the words yellow and streak are in the same phrase, weakness, cowardly or spineless is implied. It is never a compliment and always demeaning.

Example:

- The yellow streak down his back matched his running shoes; he's a total coward.

Ax to grind

Someone who has "an ax to grind" has a grudge. Something has been bothering him and he needs to tell others about it.

Example:

- He had an ax to grind with cat owners so he targeted his virus for all websites that contained the word cat.

Backseat driver

A "backseat driver" means a person who is merely trying to control a situation.

Example:

- Oh, great. We have two backseat drivers.

Back to the drawing board

It means that a plan or idea failed and a person needs to rework the plan in order to succeed.

Example:

Plan A did not work. I was hoping that Plan A would work. I don't have any other plans in mind. Now I must go back to the drawing board and make new and better plans.

Back to the old grind

It means you are going back to work after a break or lunch.

Example:

- After a long time I am back to the old grind.

Banker's hours

To use the phrase "banker's hours" is to suggest or imply that a person does not adhere to regular business hours.

Example:

Call before you go there. He keeps banker's hours.

Bargain basement prices

"Bargain basement prices" are prices that are extremely low.

Example:

- The ad says that they had bargain basement prices.

Barking orders

"Barking orders" are simply commands. Usually these orders are spoken harshly. This is what he needs to do. These are the commands he must follow.

Example:

- I received my barking orders but didn't like it.

Barrel of laughs

A barrel of laughs simply means that something is a lot of fun. A person or activity can be a barrel of laughs.

Example:

- When we were riding the roller coaster, we had a barrel of laughs.

Beat a path to his door

This phrase can be used in the positive or negative. It means a person is eager to do something.

Example:

People are beating a path to his door to buy that product

Bent out of shape

Usually people get "bent out of shape" when things don't

go their way. They become angry and frustrated, but it goes beyond that. Their anger does not match the reason why they became angry.

Example:

- Don't get so bent out of shape. It's only a piece of paper.

Better late than never

This phrase usually applies to a person or situation that is late. It can be a sarcastic reply to the late person.

Example:

- Ah welcome you are better late than never.

Beyond a shadow of a doubt

This idiom is used every single day in a variety of instances. The phrase "beyond a shadow of a doubt" means that you are absolutely sure about something.

Example:

- I know beyond a shadow of a doubt that he took my watch.

Bible thumper

A Bible thumper is a derogatory term for somebody who goes around with the Bible in his hand and is obnoxious about telling people that they need to get right with God.

Example:

- Fortunately not all Christians are Bible thumpers.

Big Daddy Warbucks

"Big Daddy Warbucks" refers to a person who has "deep pockets" to take care of financial problems that arise.

Example:

- Big Daddy Warbucks is only a phone call away.

Big shot

A "big shot" is someone who is important. Perhaps it is better to say it is someone that someone else thinks is important.

Example:

- **He thinks he's a big shot, but nobody really knows who he is.**

Big time

If you really want to do something, you might use "big time" for emphasis.

Example:

- I wanted to go to see this movie tonight. Big time.

Bite the bullet

It means that you must do what you have to do even though it is costly and time consuming.

Example:

- He didn't want to get his tooth removed because it was expensive but he had to bite the bullet to get it removed.

Black and white

A "black-and-white issue" is something that is very clear in meaning. There is no gray in the meaning.

Example:

- It is wrong to murder somebody. This is a black-and-white issue everybody agrees with.

Blind-side someone

To "blind-side someone" is to hit him when he isn't looking or when he isn't expecting it. It can be a physical hit or it can be a verbal hit. When someone blind-sides you verbally, he says something negative that you aren't expecting.

Example:

- I got my car repaired from the mechanic and he has just blind-sided me with the bill.

Blown out of the water

An idea that is "blown out of the water" means that it was a bad idea.

Example:

- Several project members blew my new project out of the water.

Blue collar worker

A "blue collar worker" is somebody who works in a factory, as a mechanic, or generally uses his hands in a job. A blue collar worker does not work in an office. The term comes from the uniforms that men used to wear when they worked in a factory.

Example:

- Yesterday I went to a factory and saw many blue collar workers there.

Booked up solid

We "book" things all the time. We book an airline ticket, hotel, car rental, or theater tickets. If something is booked up solid, it means there is absolutely no way you can obtain a ticket.

Example:

- We arrived too late. The restaurant was booked up solid.

Booming business

A "booming business" is a business that is doing very well. An economy can be booming.

Example:

- To create a booming business requires patience, endurance and hard workers.

Bored to pieces

This means that a person is very bored.

Example:

- I was bored to pieces after doing my homework.

Born with a silver spoon in his mouth

If someone is "born with a silver spoon in his mouth" it means that he was born into a wealthy family. He has everything provided for him and he has not had to work for a living.

Example:

- My school principal was born with a silver spoon in his mouth.

Bottled up all day

If you are "bottled up all day" it means that you are sitting around inside with nowhere to go.

Example:

- I was bottled up all day with my Science project.

Bottom dropped out

When the "bottom drops out" of something it implies that you have lost control of it.

Example:

- A lot of people were trying to get out of the market when the buildings had bottom dropped out.

Bottom line

It means the main point.

Example:

- The bottom line is that I really don't want to go out tonight.

Brand spanking new

It means new. That's all, new. It has never been used before.

Example:

- This dress is brand spanking new, right off the showroom rack.

Break down and buy it

- When someone says that they "broke down and bought" something, it means that they have wanted to buy it for some time now but because of low finances, they have not been able to afford it.

Example:

- I need to buy a car but I have to break down and buy it.

Break the ice

- "Breaking the ice" is ways of getting to know people you don't know.

Example:

- We need to find a way to break the ice here.

Bring back the good old days

- "The good old days" are the way things were that seemed better. Every generation thinks their generation was the best and when they look back they call them "the good old days."

Example:

- Everyone wants to bring back the good old days of childhood.

Bring down the house

- Usually performers "bring down the house" with their outstanding performances. When a person brings down the house, people are generally pleasantly surprised at the performance.

Example:

- She brought down the house with her soothing voice.

Buckle down and study

- Buckling down has the meaning of getting serious. Perhaps the child must now work harder.

Example:

- Mom says I need to buckle down and study if I want to get into college.

Bum rap

"A bum rap" is someone who has been falsely accused of something. The person has been misjudged.

Example:

- The business owner thought I had stolen from the store. I didn't take anything and I got a bum rap.

Burn the candle at both ends

When someone "burns the candle at both ends" he is working night and day to get something accomplished or to earn more money.

Example:

- If you want to pass the exam, you'll have toburn out quickly by burning the candle at both ends.

Burn up the keyboard

Someone who "burns up the keyboard" is a very fast typist. Sometimes it is used in jest of someone who might be very slow.

Example:

- Wow, you're really burning up the keyboard!

Burning a hole in his pocket

For some people money does not last long in a person's wallet or "pocket," so when the money is "burning a hole is his pocket," he wants to spend it. He is not the type of person who saves money.

Example:

- I gave him a five dollar bill this morning and I know it's burning a hole in his pocket.

Called on the carpet

If you get "called on the carpet" you are in trouble.

Example:

- I was called on the carpet for cheating on the test.

Call it a day

When you "call it a day" you are finished working. This is usually said by the person in charge of a project.

Example:

- When you finish cleaning the room, let's call it a day.

Can you handle it?

It means can you do all the work that is necessary to complete it.

Example:

- I have a task for you. It is a large task and may take you several days to accomplish. Can you handle it?"

Carry out an order

This simply means to accomplish something or to finish it.

Example:

- I don't like it when new recruits can't carry out simple orders.

Catch a cold

A "cold" in this phrase means bad coughing, fever, and chills.

Example:

- Button up or you'll catch a cold.

Catch my second wind

When a person "catches his second wind" he is refreshed and ready to work hard again. It implies that now that he's rested, he can complete what he started.

Example:

- I needed that nap. Now I've got to catch my second wind.

Catch the bus

A person "catches the bus" by being ready when the bus pulls up. It can also mean that a person has looked at the bus schedule and knows when the bus will arrive. He will be there when it arrives.

Example:

- If you get there by 7:05, you'll catch the bus.

Catch wind

The simple definition for "catch wind of" is heard. Probably you overheard it.

Example:

- I caught wind that you will be entering the contest.

Caught with his pants down

If someone is "caught with his pants down," he has been caught doing something unexpectedly that he shouldn't have been doing.

Example:

- When the guests arrived we were caught with our pants down as we weren't prepared for them to be with us for the weekend.

Chew the fat

It means people have no agenda when they talk. Maybe it's the weather or politics or sports or whatever comes to mind. There is no goal except for being social.

Example:

- We were sitting under the tree and chewing the fat.

Chip off the old block

"A chip off the old block" is somebody who is like somebody else, usually a relative. If a person is a chip off the old block he's usually like his father in speech or action.

Example:

- Every day, he's becoming more and more a chip off the old block.

Chipper

To be "chipper" means to be happy.

Example:

- Why are you so chipper today?

Clean someone's clock

You have hit a person hard, usually in the head, if you "clean his clock."

Example:

- I really cleaned his clock after he insulted me.

Clear cut

A "clear cut" is a very clear issue.

Example:

- The decision to build our own home was clear cut as there was no alternative.

Clock watcher

The words "clock watcher" implies that a person is always watching the clock or his watch because he wants to leave quickly. If he has a 9-5 job, he will leave promptly at five o'clock, not a minute more.

Example:

- I wish he'd spend more time as an employee as he does as a clock watcher.

Close call

A close call means that somebody barely avoided in an accident.

Example:

- Tom threw the ball to Jim. I ducked my head just in time. That was a close call.

Coast is clear

The "coast is clear" is another way of saying, "all clear." Nothing is in the way of you proceeding.

Example:

- If a truck is backing up and needs help, a person behind the car may say, "the coast is clear." It is now okay to back up.

Cocky

If you are "cocky," you are arrogant and extremely confident, annoyingly so.

Example:

- He thought he was so cocky when he won the championship.

Coin a new phrase

To "coin a new phrase" is to bring it into existence. New phrases are introduced and coined every year.

Example:

- Many phrases are introduced into language but few are truly coined.

Cold cash

"Cold cash" is cash, real currency. It is stated specifically instead of credit cards or checks.

Example:

- He paid me back, $1000 in cold cash.

Cold comment

"Cold comments" are unkind and uncaring words. Anything that is cold is often harsh.

Example:

- "I hope you fall and break your leg!" "Wow. That was a cold comment."

Come hell or high water

The phrase "come hell or high water" means that it doesn't matter what happens, I'll do what I said I would do.

Example:

- Nothing will prevent me from doing this. Come hell or high water, I will be at the party.

Come to grips with

This phrase means to try to understand why something happened.

Example:

- When I heard the story then I tried to come to grips.

Corner on the market

You have a corner on the market when you have no competition and are not likely to get any competition.

Example:

- If anybody buys a turtle-shaped table and only you sell turtle-shaped tables, you have a corner on the market.

Corner on the truth

When you have a "corner on the truth," only you have the truth. A person does not say that he has a corner on the truth, but other people comment that he thinks he has a corner on the truth.

Example:

- I can't believe he actually said that! Does he really think that he has a corner on the truth?

Cover your backside

It means to protect yourself against people who might want to use something you said or did against you.

Example:

- You've always got to cover your backside when dealing with those people.

Crack the books

To "crack the books" literally means to open them. When a book is new, you might hear a crackling sound when you first open it.

Example:

- Sorry I can't go to the party tonight. I need to crack the books.

Crack under pressure

When someone cracks under pressure, he reveals information that he normally would not reveal. Criminals crack under pressure when law enforcement officials need information.

Example:

- He is cracking under pressure.

Cramp my style

This is a phrase that isn't used much anymore. It means to hinder the way a person does something.

Example:

- If someone were to tell me that critics didn't like the way I sang a song, I might respond, "I don't care. It doesn't cramp my style."

Crank up the music

"Cranking up the music" means simply to turn it up loud,

really loud. We might also use crank with the word "volume."

Example:

- Crank up the music. It's party time.

Crash course

A "crash course" can be one course or a series of courses on the essentials of a topic. A crash course is not an official course and it is very informal.

Example:

- I took a crash course on "how to plant a garden."

Cry all the way to the bank

Someone who "cries all the way to the bank" isn't concerned about what others say or do to him because he is profiting. In the end, he will cash a check. The person is profiting financially.

Example:

- A reporter was talking to Raj's brother about a rumor concerning his brother. Raj's brother responded, "I'm sure he's crying about that all the way to the bank."

Crystal clear

"Crystal clear" means obvious or transparent.

Example:

- It's crystal clear to me what happened now that you confessed.

Cut and dried

If something is "cut and dried" it is clear cut. There is no middle ground or "gray area" as I've discussed earlier in the phrase "black and white issue."

Example:

- The case against her was cut and dried.

Cut me some slack

If you "cut someone some slack," you are "going easy" on them. Your rules may not be as strict with them for various reasons.

Example:

- Why didn't you clean your room like I asked you to?"

  "Oh Mom, cut me some slack. I mowed the lawn and cleaned my room. That should account for something."

Day in and day out

Simply, this phrase means every single day.

Example:

- He jogs three miles day in and day out.

Day late and a dollar short

This phrase usually means that a person or organization is late in completing a project. This idiom deals with lateness. It rarely deals with money, despite the reference to a dollar. It means late and /or not a quality completion.

Example:

- If I invent something that was invented two months

ago, someone might say that I was "a day late and a dollar short."

Deadbeat

A "deadbeat" is someone who is considered lazy.

Example:

- The Courts have helped mothers pursue deadbeat dads.

Dead end

"Dead ends" in everyday language are roads that have no "outlets." The roads go nowhere. You must drive back the same way you came in order to travel on different roads. In fact, a common yellow sign is a sign that reads: "Dead End: No outlet." Dead end issues are those that can go nowhere.

Example:

- Our discussion was a dead end.

Dead in the water

If something is "dead in the water" it is finished before it got a chance to get started. It was doomed to fail before getting started.

Example:

- Why did we even start that project? It was dead in the water from day one?

Dead issue

"Dead issues" are those that can "go nowhere." It often relates to facts that are no longer significant.

Example:

- Why does he persist in bringing up those faulty statistics? It's a dead issue?

Dead ringer

A "dead ringer" refers to a person who looks like someone else.

Example:

- He's a dead ringer for his dad.

Deal and a half

A "deal and a half" is a transaction that is very good, usually for the buyer.

Example:

- If I purchase a book, the store owner might say to me, "I'll not only sell you this for 50 rupees, but I'll throw in two other books into the deal." To me, that's a deal and a half.

Decked out

A "decked out" person is someone who is really dressed well, normally for a special occasion. Parties and events can also be decked out with decorations.

Example:

- Everyone was decked out at Trisha's party.

Dig his own grave

The phrase "digging his own grave" means that a person,

by his own words and actions, is causing himself greater harm than is necessary.

Example:

- Honey admitted to taking the hammer from the store. He's just digging his own grave.

Dime a dozen

It means you can find things easily. They are in good supply.

Example:

- Writers in most major cities are a dime a dozen.

Dirt cheap

This is something that is very inexpensive.

Example:

- He bought that computer dirt cheap.

Dirt poor

If a family is dirt poor, they have very little money. They are worse than poor.

Example:

- We didn't have much money while I was growing up. We might have even been considered dirt poor.

Do that in your sleep

This idiom means to be able to do something without thinking about it. You've done it so much that you don't need to think about it. If you were sleeping you could still do it.

Example:

- Somebody who works in a factory making one thing all day, every day, could make that thing in his sleep, without thought about whether he's doing it correctly or not.

Don't fence me in

This phrase means to not put borders around my speech and actions. Let me go free.

Example:

- Amit asked his governess not to fence him in.

Don't get smart with me

It is a warning to the child not to misuse his words.

Example:

- Don't get smart with me, young man!

Don't knock it

"Don't knock it" is used when something is given to you unexpectedly and someone else makes a sarcastic remark about it.

Example:

- Okay, so the car I bought is 7years old. Don't knock it. It gets me around town.

Don't let it lick you

When someone wants to console you, he may use "don't let it lick you" or "don't let it beat you." It's not the end of the world that this happened. You can "bounce" back and regain your confidence.

Example:

- Cheer up. Don't let it lick you.

Don't rattle his cage

This means the same thing as "don't make him angry." If you "rattle someone's cage," you are irritating that person. It implies that the person gets upset easily.

Example:

- He's just bluffing. Don't let him rattle your cage.

Don't sweat the small stuff

We use this phrase quite frequently. Essentially this means, "don't worry about it." If it's small, it's not that important. Worry about the large things in life instead.

Example:

- Where's that smile I like to see? Don't sweat the small stuff.

Don't try to pin that one on me

Usually this is said when someone is being accused of something and he is trying to say he didn't do it.

Example:

- You think I shot that guy? Don't try to pin that one on me.

Don't write me off

If you "write someone off," you are either ignoring them or thinking what they have to say is not important.

Example:

- I requested my instructor, "Sir, please don't write me off. I will concentrate on my coaching now."

Double take

A "double take" is a quick second look at something. It implies that you took a second, closer look. It may be an actual physical movement or it may be one that is only spoken.

Example:

- I see someone who looks like a famous actor. I would do a "double take" to make sure it really was him.

Double-crossed

Nobody likes to be "double-crossed." The best way to explain a double cross is to betray secretly.

Example:

- I didn't expect that you would double-cross me.

Down and out

"Down and out" means that a person has had a streak of bad luck. The future does not look bright for him. He is seriously depressed.

Example:

- Don't be so hard on him. He's been pretty down and out lately.

Down the road (time)

We would use "down the road" to mean sometime in the

future. Depending on the context, it could mean next week or next year.

Example:

- That's a good idea we'll have to explore down the road.

Down the tubes

If a project "goes down the tubes" it failed. There is no longer any hope that the projects will succeed.

Example:

- That project went down the tubes on the first day of its existence.

Down to the wire

If you are "down to the wire," you are probably running late for a deadline.

Example:

- I am afraid how I will score good marks as I am down to the wire for the submission of the project.

First things first

This idiom means "let's begin at the beginning." If you read off a list of 10 things that need to be done, you might say to a worker, but "first things first." It will be the first item on the list that is priority.

Example:

- We have a number of projects we need to work on but first things first, the plumbing.

Fisticuffs

If an argument descends into "fisticuffs," punches are thrown. Fisticuffs mean that physical contact was made. They were truly fighting.

Example:

- Their argument went beyond words and into fisticuffs.

Fit to be tied

A person or group of people can be "fit to be tied." They are extremely angry. Something happened and they do not like it…at all.

Example:

- When he heard that his new BMW was smashed, he was fit to be tied?

Flash in the pan

A "flash in the pan" is a person or organisation that has a lot of promise initially, but it was only for a short time period.

Example:

- We'll have to wait to see if Google is just another flash in the pan or a viable company.

Flood pants

"Flood pants" are long pants that are too short. The pants do not extend to the shoes. This is becoming less popular as clothing designers are designing shorter pants and calling it the newest fashion.

Example:

- I see you're wearing flood pants this morning.

Fly-by-night

You do not want to associate with a "fly by night" organisation. It is not credible. You do not want to give money to a "fly by night" because they may not be there in the morning.

Example:

- That company has changed its name six times in the past 4 months. It's clearly a fly by night operation.

For the life of me

This idiom simply means, "I've tried and tried and tried, but for the life of me, I cannot do it." It means I'm giving up trying or trying to understand.

Example:

- For the life of me I don't understand why he likes her.

Fountain of youth

The older you get, the more likely you are to search for "the fountain of youth." Supposedly if you drink from that fountain you will never get old.

Example:

- My grandparents are always searching for the fountain of youth.

From rags to riches

This phrase is often used to describe a person who went

from poverty to wealth over the course of a lifetime. Rags to riches stories can also happen quickly.

Example:

- His is truly a rag to riches story.

Frustrated to no end

Another way to put this phrase is "there was no end to my frustration." They are identical in meaning.

Example:

- That hardware problem frustrated me to no end.

Get a load of him

A simpler way to use this phrase is "would you look at him!" Perhaps he does something the hard way and two people are watching him. If he would have used a machine to lift it, it would have been a lot easier. It can be used about someone trying to get attention.

Example:

- "Get a load of him. He thinks he's Superman."

Get a move on it

"Move faster. Go faster." Both are different ways to say "get a move on it."

Example:

- What's the matter, Raman? What are you waiting for? Get a move on it.

Get a word in edgewise

If someone talks a lot, it is often difficult to "get a word in edgewise." Edgewise means if you put the word the on its edge like this you will be able to squeeze in talk. It is the inability to break into a conversation.

Example:

- I couldn't get a word in edgewise.

Get down to brass tacks

"Let's get down to brass tacks" is a way of saying, let's get to the "heart of the matter," the important things. There may be a hundred details but there are probably only one or two really important things. These are the brass tacks.

Example:

- Let's get down to brass tacks. How much money are we talking about here?

Get it off the ground

This phrase means to begin a project. Getting major projects off the ground can be difficult because there are many details to workout. But once it is off the ground, then we can evaluate where the project is. The most important thing, though, is getting it started.

Example:

- Once we get this company off the ground, we'll talk about other businesses we'd like to start.

Get on the horn

"The horn" is slang for the telephone.

Example:

- Get on the horn and call my accountant.

Get on with it

"Get on with it" is as simple as "let's continue" or "let's start." It depends on the context. Often it is said impatiently.

Example:

- We need to finish this before leaving. Let's get on with it.

Get out there pounding pavement

"Pounding the pavement" can be as simple as knocking on doors or telephoning potential customers. It is generally related to sales. If sales are down, salesmen are asked to get out pounding the pavement. This phrase is also used to tell someone to go look for employment.

Example:

- When the orders stopped coming in, the boss suggested we might want to get out and pound the pavement?

Get something for a song

You probably got a really good deal if you "got something for a song." It means that the person selling the item was almost giving it away. This is especially true when the item is normally very expensive.

Example:

- It was an estate sale; we got the artwork for a song.

Get the green light

If you ever "get the green light" for a project, you've been given permission to start it.

Example:

- We got the green light to go ahead with the software revision.

Get the hang of it

When you "get the hang of it," you are finally doing something well that you've never done before. You might even say to yourself and others that "Hey, I'm getting the hang of this."

Example:

- If I've never used a hammer and after an hour I am pounding nails into boards skillfully, I am finally getting the hang of using a hammer.

Get the lead out

If someone tells you to "get the lead out" it means that they are in a rush to get something done. Since lead is heavy, freeing yourself from lead will enable you to move faster. It's another way of saying "hurry up!"

Example:

- She was in the bathroom for 30 minutes applying makeup. I told her to get the lead out because others wanted to use it.

Give it a go/shot

This simply means "try it" or to try it once.

Example:

- Give it a shot. It can't hurt (to try it).

Give me a buzz

Simply, this means to call me on the telephone.

Example:

- When you get back home, give me a buzz to let me know you made it there safely?

Give me the low down

"Give me the low down" means to tell me the story and the details. I want it all.

Example:

- What happened with Fred while I was gone? Give me the low down?

Give someone a line

When you are accused of "giving someone a line" you are being accused of lying?

Example:

- Stop giving me a line. I am fed up of your excuses.

Give someone a piece of my mind

Often when a person is angry, she will "give him a piece of her mind." Basically she will tell him what she thinks of him, the situation and a few more things that he may or may not have control over. We would say she is just "venting" her anger and frustrations.

Example:

- I was ready to give him a piece of my mind when the phone rang.

Give you a run for your money

When you give someone "a run for their money," you are putting up a good fight. You never gave up even when it would have been easy to do so. You may lose but you still gave them a run for their money.

Example:

- I may be the smallest bidder, but I'll give them a run for their money.

Glued to the TV

Kids are often glued to the television set. They are not literally attached. But the shows are interesting enough to attract their interest for a long period of time. They seemed to be inseparable.

Example:

- I was glued to the TV for the entire hour.

God forsaken place

This is a fairly common phrase used to describe a place that you do not want to go because it is so terrible. The implication in this idiom is very clear: even God has left this place. Why would you want to go there? We might say it about a country, a city, or a neighbourhood.

Example:

- I couldn't wait to leave that God forsaken place.

Go for all the gusto

This phrase means to put all your strength into a project. Give it everything you have. Don't hold back.

Example:

- Go for all the gusto. A very popular col drink commercial year ago used this as a slogan. "In everything you do, go for all the gusto."

Go-getter

A "go-getter" is similar to "a fireball." It is used to describe a person who is very energetic and someone who gets things done.

Example:

- She's a real go-getter.

Goldbricker

A "goldbricker" is someone who fakes illness. It is never a compliment. It is sometimes used in jest.

Example:

- You wouldn't be goldbricking now, would you?

Good dirt

"Do you have any good dirt" is simply another way to ask if you have any good gossip. You are trying to get "dirt" about someone else. We might even ask for "juicy gossip."

Example:

- You have any good dirt about that company?

Good for what ails you

If something is "good for what ails you," it means that it's good for you in your time of need. It is a difficult phrase to define because it is so general.

Example:

- Herbal tea, a massage, healthy food, clean living are all good for what ails you.

Go with the flow

"Go with the flow" means to do what everyone else is doing. Fit in. Don't be different.

Example:

- If you want to survive at this company, you must go with the flow.

Grab some lunch

This is a phrase you would say when you want to eat a quick lunch. You might even use the words "quick lunch." You are working with a few guys and you are at a point in your project that you can take a break.

Example:

- Let's grab some lunch before we tackle the next portion."

Grasp for straws

If a person is "grasping for straws," he is searching for bits of information he can hold onto in order to validate his point. Usually the bits of information are weak.

Example:

- Rohan was grasping at straws to prove his statement.

How much does that run?

This phrase simply means how much does it cost?

Example:

- How much is a new Pentium IV computer running for these days?

Hunker down

We don't use this phrase much anymore. It means to make sure the details are completed. It means to get the job done, whatever it takes. We might also say "bear down."

Example:

- We need to hunker down and put full effort into it.

I can't make heads or tails of this

This phrase means that either you can't read it because it is too small or you can't understand it because the wording is bad. Usually product documentation is like this. In fact, this kind of documentation is unreadable and not understandable.

Example:

- Who wrote this garbage? I can't make heads or tails of this?

I can't stand ...

This idiom means "I don't like this at all." If you can't

stand something, probably you hate it. We apply this to people, situations, and things.

Example:

- I can't stand it when people drive slowly.

I didn't sleep a wink

If a person doesn't sleep a wink at night, it means that he has a lot of trouble sleeping at night. It is merely hyperbole.

Example:

- I need coffee this morning. I couldn't sleep a wink all night.

I don't know him from Adam

When you "don't know someone from Adam," it means that you do not know this person at all. How can you possibly trust him if you don't know him?

Example:

- If my car breaks down along the road and somebody stops to help me, my first thought is "how can I trust this person to help me? I don't know him from Adam?"

I don't speak his language

Programmers speak a different language. Engineers speak a different language. Business people speak a different language. When a business person says that he does not speak the programmers' language, he is accurate. They use different words to describe different events.

Example:

- I've been trying to talk to the mechanic but I really don't speak his language.

I hate to break the news

This phrase is almost always followed by the word "but." It means that I do not want to be the one to tell you the bad news. However, because I have the news, I will tell you the news. It will not be good news.

Example:

- If I hear a rumor at work that my coworker will be losing his job, I might take him aside and say, "you know Bill, I hate to break the news to you but I've been hearing rumors lately about the need to cut jobs..."

I haven't a clue

Simply put, "I haven't a clue" means "I don't know." Similarly, if someone refers to another as "clueless," it means he doesn't know and he does not have the capacity to know.

Example:

- I haven't a clue what he's talking about.

I haven't the foggiest

This phrase has lost its popularity but you will hear it occasionally. It is identical to "I haven't a clue."

Example:

- I haven't the foggiest idea what he just said. Was it English?

If opportunity knocks...

To finish this phrase, "if opportunity knocks, open the door." It means that if you have an opportunity you should take advantage of it. It is there now but it may not be there tomorrow. You might only hear the words written above.

Example:

- They wanted to pay you how much? Hey man, if opportunity knocks...

If push comes to shove

When a person or organisation is in a difficult position it may be forced to make tough decisions that would affect you personally?

Example:

- Companies will make mistakes but when "push comes to shove," they will do what is best for the company and not the needs of the individual.

If worse comes to worse

This is a phrase we say when we will do what it takes when the time comes.

Example:

- If I were to lose my job and have no income for five months, I may say, "if worse comes to worse, I can always move away to live in a cheaper area."

Kick him when he's down

This phrase means to hurt someone after he has fallen or failed.

Example:

- If I make major mistakes on a project, the boss might come to me and ask me why I'm such an idiot. I'm already upset that I made mistakes. He is kicking me when I'm down. He is also "adding insult to injury," another idiom we'll discuss.

Kick ideas around

This phrase simply means to put a few related or unrelated ideas out and to discuss them. The thought is to see which idea makes the most sense.

Example:

- Let's meet next week to kick a few ideas around.

Knock off work

This phrase simply means to quit working for the day.

Example:

- The boss ordered to knock off the work.

Knock someone's lights out

If you "knock someone's lights out" you have hit that person hard, probably in the face or head.

Example:

- If he ever touches my son, I'll knock his lights out.

Know this inside and out

This phrase means to know something thoroughly. You are to know it from "cover to cover." Sometimes it is course or subject material. It is very close to actually memorizing the material.

Example:

- The coach says to his players, "here is the playbook. You have one week to know this inside and out. If you don't, you won't play."

Last ditch effort

A "last ditch effort" is the final attempt someone will make to complete an action. It is the last thing they will do before giving up. After this, the person will try something else a new way.

Example:

- He apologised. It was a last ditch effort to save the relationship.

Last straw

The full phrase to this is "this is the straw that broke the camel's back." The idea behind this is that a camel can carry a lot. If you overload the camel it will break his back. Similarly, a person can only handle so much. He too has a breaking point. The last straw is that breaking point. Often we shorten the expression to "the last straw."

Example:

- This was the last straw. Either you go or I go. Which is it?

Latest rage

The "latest rage" is the newest thing on the market that

everybody is talking about or buying. Typically it applies to clothing or electronics.

Example:

- The latest rage will anger many parents because it is so expensive.

Laughing stock

Everyone is laughing at you if you are the "laughing stock." You have made a fool of yourself. We also use this even if people aren't laughing at you out loud. It means that you have embarrassed yourself or your organisation.

Example:

- When David arrived at the meeting wearing shorts, he made a laughing stock of himself and the company?

Lay all your cards on the table

When you "lay all your cards on the table," you are telling all the facts for people to see?

Example:

- My brother laid all his cards on the table to prove his innocence.

Lay down the law

Parents "lay down the law" regularly. In essence, they say, "these are the rules you must live by. If you choose not to live by them, live somewhere else." A judge can also lay down the law by saying, "this is the law and I'm going to uphold it. You will go to jail now."

Example:

- Mr. Mills laid down the law: no boyfriends until she's 16 years old.

Lay it all on the line

To "lay something all on the line" means to either give it all you have or to give all the information you have at once.

Example:

- When the police asked me where I was that night, I laid it all on the line for them for the past two weeks?

Lay low for a while

To "lay low for a while," means to not draw a lot of attention to yourself.

Example:

- I made three major mistakes at work today and I think I need to lay low for a while until the boss cools down.

Leap for joy

When someone "leaps for joy," they are extremely happy? The person does not leap physically but they probably could becausethey are so happy.

Example:

- When I found out it was a baby girl, I leaped for joy?

Off the hook

If you are "let off the hook," you will be thankful. It means that no one is holding you responsible for actions.

You are no longer a" suspect." This can even apply to the family.

Examples:

- Jamie confessed to breaking the vase. So, I'm letting
- Mary off the hook.

Off the wall

If someone makes a statement that is "off the wall," it is an unusual statement. It is weird and doesn't make sense.

Example:

- If I were to ask you to spell the capital of Cleveland," you'd respond (hopefully) that my question was "off the wall because Cleveland is not a state. People can be off the wall too.

Oldest trick in the book

This is an expression someone says when he's been fooled by someone when he should have known better. We would say "he fell for it" or "he fell for the oldest trick in the book."

Example:

- One of my "tricks" is to approach a person from behind, tap him on the left shoulder and move to his right side. When he turns to the left, he realizes that he fell for one of the oldest tricks in the book. It is something that a child might do. It keeps me young.

Oldie but goodie

This expression is used to indicate something that is older

but still valid as a form of expression. Typically, this relates to music tha tis older.

Example:

- I heard an "oldie but goodie" the other day on the radio."

On a kick

If a person emphasizes one thing for a length of time, he is "on a kick." It's like a hobby. The person is excited about something but you think he'll grow tired of it. It implies that he changes "kicks" often.

Example:

- Jim's latest kick is collecting stamps. He's been doing it now for three years.

On a roll

If someone is "on a roll" you don't want to stop him. He is making progress and is still excited about it.

Example:

- Jim painted the back half of the house and he didn't want to stop because he was on a roll."

On a shoestring

To do something "on a shoestring" means that you have very little money and you must watch every penny you spend.

Example:

- Parents always tell their children to be on a shoestring.

Run it into the ground

If you "run something into the ground," you have destroyed it. It is no longer functional.

Example:

- I can't believe it. The project was going so well until Fred started managing it. He ran it right into the ground.

Run of the mill

"Run of the mill" means ordinary. It is similar to "ordinary garden variety."

Example:

- Yesterday I bought an ordinary, run of the mill cook book.

Save it for a rainy day

When you saves omething "for a rainy day" you are simply saving it so that you can use it later. Usually you save money for a rainy day, for a time when money is not coming in as it is now.

Example:

- We need to put away a little money every month, to save it for a rainy day.

Scare the living daylights out of

This phrase is used when you really frighten someone. There is a harsher version of this phrase as well.

Example:

- He intentionally scared the living daylights out of me.

Scared stiff

Similar to the previous expression, someone who is scared stiff is immobilised because of his fear. This has a broader meaning also. It means to be worried.

Example:

- We were scared stiff about the outcome of the surgery.

Scarf it down

If you "scarf something down," you eat it quickly. It is slang and informal.

Example:

- We were in a hurry so we scarfed down the hamburger and left.

Scrap that project

When you "scrap a project," you have determined that it is not worth your time or resources to finish it. It is unfinished. You can also scrap ideas.

Example:

- The project was just costing us too much to continue, so we scrapped it.

Scrape the bottom of the barrel

When a person "scrapes the bottom of the barrel," he is getting the worst possible choice he could get. The bottom of the barrel tends to be where the junk or unwanted material settles.

Example:

- If he is selecting a job candidate, he will choose the worst candidate instead of the best. When they hired that guy who has no experience, they were really scraping the bottom of the barrel.

Scratch the surface

When you "scratch the surface," you are merely touching upon a topic. You have not done in depth analysis. You have just started to explore the topic.

Example:

- It's clear that the organisation is corrupt. I think we're just scratching the surface as to the level of corruption.

Scream bloody murder

This phrase simply means a loud shriek or excessive complaining over something small.

Example:

- When I touched her hand, she screamed bloody murder. I had not realised that she didn't like to be touched?

Search high and low

This means "I searched and I searched and I searched." Whatever I was looking for couldn't be found.

Example:

- I searched high and low for my contact lenses until I realised that I was wearing them.

Search with a fine-toothed comb

This is a thorough, detailed search.

Example:

- I searched the room with a fine-toothed comb looking for my watch.

Second fiddle

To play or to be "second fiddle" means that you are not good enough to be the best. You are not bad. You are just not the best. It also can mean that you are always striving to improve and want to advance.

Example:

- It's tough playing second fiddle, but the boss will be retiring in two years. Then I'll have my chance.

Sell yourself short

This expression is usually used in the negative. If someone tells you "don't sell yourself short," she is telling you that you have skills that should not be overlooked. It is often in response to a person's low self-esteem.

Example:

- I've seen you work. Don't sell yourself short. You can do that job.

Send a boy to do a man's job

This is often said in a joking manner. It means to have someone weaker performing a job that a stronger person should do.

Example:

- If I am opening a bottle of ketchup but can't do it, someone shakes his head and says, "they send a boy to do a man's job." At which point he will take the bottle from me and twist it off.

Set the record straight

This expression is used when a problem has occurred and someone wants to clarify the events leading up to the problem. He possibly wants to make sure that everyone understands that he wasn't at fault.

Example:

- I think I need to set the record straight here. I was out of the office when the incidents occurred.

Shady character

Someone who is shady has questionable character. You are not sure if you should trust him or not. And this might even be before you ever meet him! If someone tells you that a person is shady, run far from him.

Example:

- Look at him! He just looks shady to me.

Shaker and a mover

A "shaker and mover" is very similar to a "go-getter" and "a fireball." This term is more emphatic than the previous two terms. It means that the person stops at nothing to make things happen.

Example:

- Look for him to be a CEO ten years from now. He's a shaker and a mover.

Shape up or ship out

When someone tells you that "you either need to shape up or ship out" there are problems. You are one of those problems. Probably your behavior or your language is the problem. The phrase means to get your behavior together or leave.

Example:

- I am tired of you always staying out all night. You need to either shape up or ship out.

Shoe leather express

This means to go by foot. It's a fun way to say by foot.

Example:

- How are you getting to school? Shoe leather express?

Shyster

This also is a term for a "shady character." He is slick and smooth in presentation. He is dishonest and a "con man." He has a bad reputation.

Example:

- 2000 rupees for this sweater? What a shyster?

Sick and tired of

We use this phrase quite often. You will definitely hear it.

It means to have a very strong dislike or hatred for something that happens repeatedly or overemphasised.

Example:

- I am sick and tired of all the slow drivers in the left lane of a highway. I am sick and tired of all the people who use the phrase sick and tired.

Sidekick

A "sidekick" is someone who is one person's assistant.

Example:

- "Who's the sidekick you have there?" Oh, that's my little helper?

Sign your life away

When someone signs for a large loan or enlists in the military, he is said to be "signing his life away?" It means to sign something that has a long-term commitment. We might also use it sarcastically.

Example:

- When I bought the stereo on credit, I had to sign my life away?

Sit down and take a load off

This phrase is only used when a person who has been working or walking or running a long time comes in and looks physically exhausted.

Example:

- Sit down and take a load off. Rest a bit.

Sitting pretty

"Sitting pretty" is a very different phrase from the previous expression. This means that you are doing very well, especially financially. Or it means you have accomplished something and are far in front of your competitors.

Example:

- When we got the contract for $1 million, we were sitting pretty?

Sky's the limit

The "sky's the limit" is an extremely popular phrase in America. It simply means there are no limits; you can have whatever you want.

Example:

- Choose any place in the world you want to go to; the sky's the limit.

Slap a ticket on someone

We might also hear "slap a fine" for this phrase. This means that a policeman has issued you a ticket. There was probably no argument. You were clearly doing something wrong.

Example:

- If you speed through that neighborhood, the cops will slap a ticket on you so fast..."

Slew of things

A "slew" is a lot. The term can be used with anything with a large number in it.

Example:

- There were a slew of birds in the park today.

Slip of the tongue

A "slip of the tongue" is something you say but you do not mean to say.

Example:

- That comment was the slip of my tongue.

Slip through the cracks

If you think about the words, "slipping through the cracks," it will make sense metaphorically. If someone has slipped or fallen through the cracks, he has fallen away from people who can now help. It means the person has been forgotten or was neglected.

Example:

- The medical system is here to help people. Some people, because of their circumstances, are not able to get the care they need and fall through the cracks.

Smart Alec

A "smart Alec" is someone who is sarcastic and slightly witty.

Example:

- Don't be a smart Alec. Just give me the address for the beauty shop.

Smoke and mirrors

This simply means deception through confusion.

Example:

- The Government often uses smoke and mirrors especially when it comes to raising their own salaries. They will put the proposal in an obscure bill and pass the bill at midnight.

Sock it to 'em

The idea behind this idiom is to pursue someone or something (not romantically). It doesn't have to be physical. It is an older phrase. Perhaps an updated version of this is "you go, girl." It means to get revenge.

Example:

- It's great that you're fighting back. Sock it to 'em. They deserve it.

Something to boot (else)

This phrase means "something extra" or "in addition to" It's hard to describe until you've heard it several times. Fortunately, you will hear it several times.

Example:

- Not only did I get a free car wash with my fill up, but I got a hat to boot.

Spic and Span

Spic and Span is a brand name for a household cleaner in America. It was really popular 30 years ago. So, when someone wants you to make the room Spic and Span, they want you to clean it thoroughly.

Example:

- After I was done, my room was Spic and Span.

Spit it out

If a person is having a hard time forming or articulating an idea, he will be encouraged to "come on, spit it out." It is said in a joking manner.

Example:

- He spits out comments about every person.

Spittin' image

You can substitute the following words for this phrase and it will mean the same thing: "he looks exactly like him."

Example:

- He's the spittin' image of his old man (slang for father).

Spur of the moment

This is something, usually an idea, you have but you haven't thought it through fully.

Example:

- His spur of the moment idea turned out to be very profitable.

Squirrelly

If you are acting "squirrelly," you are unpredictable and jumpy. People can have squirrelly moods. Typically it is a short term condition. We have other words to describe someone who is squirrelly for a length of time.

Example:

- He was acting squirrelly until I found out why: he had just broken up with his friend.

Standing agreement

A "standing agreement" can be either written or oral. It is an agreement that is currently in effect. It is not a one-time agreement, but one that is ongoing.

Example:

- Don't forget. We have a standing agreement that you'll shovel the snow from October to March.

Standstill

If an activity comes to a "standstill" it has come to a temporary halt. It may or not resume depending on the circumstances.

Example:

- The traffic came to a standstill. No one was going anywhere.

Start from day one

When you "start from day one," you are beginning (perhaps a second or third time) from the first day of the project?

Example:

- We knew from day one that this project was going to succeed.

Start from scratch

When you "start from scratch," you are beginning with

no plans? You will make plans and everything associated with the project. When you make a cake "from scratch," you are using "raw materials such as eggs, flour and sugar. No pre-mixed boxes, just a recipe?

Example:

- We knew that we had to start this thing from scratch if it was to succeed.

Start from square one

This phrase is similar to "from day one" and can be used in place of it. The slight difference is that you are beginning at the beginning. It has the idea that you are starting over. Or you are just starting the project. The differences are very subtle, but the overall meaning is clear: From the start.

Example:

- After the manager left, we knew we were back to square one because he had all the ideas in his head and didn't put them on paper.

Start from the word go

This phrase generally means from the beginning. It does not specify a day in the project.

Example:

- From the word go we knew this project was doomed because of poor management.

State of the art

"State of the art" is the best, most advanced technology available.

Example:

- My office has been state of the art since I set it up. It has all the latest technology and is very comfortable.

Steal your thunder

This phrase is related to the previous idiom. When you "steal someone's thunder," you are using the words that he might use when he speaks?

Example:

- If when I'm preparing for a speech I want to emphasise a point by making a joke. The speaker before me uses the exact same joke I was planning to use. He has stolen my thunder.

Stepping stone

The phrase "a stepping stone" derives from a series of rocks in a stream that a person steps on so that he won't get his feet wet when crossing the stream. A stepping stone is one step to a larger goal.

Example:

- Going to a professional university for the professional basketball player is a stepping stone to the pros.

Stick in the mud

A "stick in the mud" usually is someone who is responsible for delaying progress on a project.

Example:

- Why are you being such a stick in the mud? We could have been finished with it days ago?

Stick it to 'em

This phrase is similar to "sock it to 'em" but it is a little more current. It has the same idea of getting even or making someone pay.

Example:

- When you get into divorce court, you need to stick it to 'em. He deserves it?

Still up in the air

This means that a decision has not yet been made.

Example:

- It's still up in the air if we're going on that long trip we've been planning,

Stone cold

This is an adjective that describes a person's condition. It means absolutely. Drunk and sober tend to be the two words associated with this adjective.

Example:

- He came to the meeting stone cold drunk.

Stop dead in your tracks

This phrase means to stop doing what you are doing immediately. It implies suddenness.

Example:

- I stopped dead in my tracks when I saw the bear ahead of me.

Stop the presses

This is a general phrase that also means to stop what you are doing.

Example:

- Whoa, whoa. Stop the presses. Give me a minute to think about this.

Stop the world and let me off

A person says this when he is confused and tired. Perhaps the day didn't go well.

Example:

- Stop the world and let me off. I just want to go to bed.

Storm on the horizon

The literal meaning to this is obvious: A storm is ready to strike. However, there is a more subtle meaning as well. It has the idea that somewhere "out there" a big unpleasant event is about to happen. Perhaps a teacher has been seeing poorer and poorer grades from his students. Maybe a parent is beginning to notice that performance as well. Something is about ready to explode. And when it explodes, it won't be pretty.

Example:

- The storm of economic doom for X country is on the horizon. You can see it in the unemployment rates, housing interest rates, and manufacturing indices.

Street smart

If you are "street smart," you know how the real world works. In a city, you would know about gangs, gang signs, and violent crimes. In the country, you might know about farming and fixing things. In the corporate world, you know about bureaucracy and office politics.

Example:

- There goes a man you should know. He's very street smart.

Straddle the fence

When a person "straddles the fence," he is indecisive. He isn't sure which way to go. He wants the best of all worlds?

Example:

- You can't straddle the fence long. You must make a decision to go with us or to go with them.

Straight forward

A person who is "straight forward," is very direct. He is direct in speech. He is direct in action. Straight forward people can be irritating. They can also be refreshing.

Example:

- I like the straight forward approach much better than beating around the bush.

Straight from the get-go

This phrase is similar to phrases we've discussed earlier. It means straight from the start. It is very informal.

Example:

- We need to do things right, right from the get-go.

Straight-laced

A person who is "straight-laced" probably doesn't drink, smoke, swear, has one wife, doesn't have a girlfriend on the side, is honest and doesn't "go out with the boys." Many would consider him boring. Some would say he is the ideal husband.

Example:

- That guy is too straight-laced for me. I need to let loose sometimes.

Strike while the iron's hot

This expression means that when something is ready, don't wait, do it now. If the opportunity becomes available, jump on it.

Example:

- You've got the money; buy the car while it's still here. It's on sale. Strike whiles the iron's hot.

Stuck on himself

This phrase is closely related to the next word, "stuck up." If someone is "stuck on himself," he is generally arrogant and thinks the world revolves around him. He is conceited.

Example:

- I can't believe how he's so stuck on himself. He thinks the world owes him favors.

Stuckup

This only describes people. People who are stuckup are arrogant and conceited. I think we actually use arrogant and conceited more than we do stuckup. It has lost meaning over the last 30 years.

Example:

- If he weren't so stuckup, he'd realise that he's no good at cricket.

Sure shot (to win)

If something is a "sure shot," it means that it will succeed. It is similar in meaning to "a shoo-in." A person or an activity can be a sure shot.

Example:

- You've got a sure shot at being the best web site out there.

Swallow your pride

"Swallowing your pride" is never easy. It simply means to be humble.

Example:

- When I was growing up, my family was on welfare for a few years? Even though I didn't like it, it was all we could do to survive the bad years. I had a hard time swallowing my pride because I thought I would never go on welfare.

Table the issue

When you "table an issue" you are putting it aside so that

you can tend to other matters. It is similar to "putting it on the backburner."

Example:

- Let's table that issue for now. We'll have time to discuss it next week.

Tables are turned

This phrase is very similar in meaning to "the joke's on you" but with differences. You are experiencing something negative whereas before, it was someone else who was experiencing it.

Example:

- You planned to have a quiet dinner a home for your birthday but your friend instead turned the tables on you and now it's a surprise party for you.

Take a back seat to

This phrase just means that something is lower in priority.

Example:

- Getting there quickly should always take a back seat to safe driving.

Take his good ol' time

A slow person "takes his good ol' time." There is no rush, no hurry.

Example:

- "Sunday drivers" take their good ol' time.

Take it easy

This is what you would say when you are saying goodbye, instead of goodbye. It is a way of saying goodbye.

Example:

- Have a safe trip? Take it easy.

Take my word for it

This is the truth so you must take my word for it. A similar phrase might be "you have my word on it" though that tends to deal with promises.

Example:

- I know what I'm talking about; take my word for it.

Take off work

"Taking off a day of work" is very common in America. It means that you call in and tell the boss that you are not working today. Also common is "taking a day off."

Example:

- I need to take off work today because my kid is ill.

Take the party line

When you "take the party line," you are saying just what the party or company or organisation would say if they were speaking. Politics is known for doing this to people. They believe something only because the party has stated it.

Example:

- You need to think for yourself and stop taking the party line.

Take your licks

When you "take your licks," you are taking the "punishment" you deserve because of what you did. The punishment does not have to be physical.

Example:

- I got in the stock market but it dropped, so I had to take my licks and get out.

Taken for a ride

If you've been "taken for a ride," you were probably swindled out of money or you bought something that was not as valuable as you thought.

Example:

- Many people on the internet get taken for a ride when they don't think about what they're doing.

Taken to the cleaners

This is the previous idiom to an extreme. If you get "taken to the cleaners," you are totally wiped out, usually financially. You have no money remaining because of your foolish actions.

Example:

- I bet all I had on number seven and was taken to the cleaners.

Talk up a blue streak

If someone is accused of "talking up a blue streak," he talks a lot.

Example:

- He talked up a blue streak but he really didn't say anything of value.

Tall order

When something is "a tall order," it is difficult to accomplish?

Example:

- Not only do I want you to finish loading all of these boxes before you go home, but those 12 over there. Response: "that sure is a tall order. But I think I'll be able to do it."

Tar and feather

It means that several people want you because of something you've done.

Example:

- That guy should be tarred and feathered for what he's done.

Taste some of your own medicine

To "taste some of your own medicine" is never good. It means that somebody does something negative to you after you did something negative to them.

Example:

- If a judge says that all non-violent thieves are to be released from prison and then he gets robbed by one of those thieves, he tastes some of his own medicine.

Tattle tale

A "tattle tale is someone who reports on someone else.

Example:

- Jasbir is pulling Soni's hair. Babita sees it and reports it to the teacher. Babita is a tattle tale.

Tear into someone

When you "tear into someone," you are yelling at them for what they've said or done? It can mean physically hitting them, but usually not.

Example:

- When I found out that my brother sold my bike, I tore into him?

Tearjerker

A "tearjerker" is a movie or book that elicits tears from the reader or movie goer. It is usually sad in the middle and will bring even the strongest of men to tears. Some authors and screenplay writers write only to please these types of audiences.

Example:

- Have you read the latest tearjerker from Danielle Steele?

Tell someone off

It means to tell someone what you really think about him and is usually negative comments. It is a face-to-face meeting.

Example:

- I overheard Terry telling Barbara off. It was loud and nasty.

Tend to the home fires

When a person is "tending to the home fires," he has decided that his life at home is more important than his professional or business career? Tending to the home fires refers to the man in charge realising that his home life is important too.

Example:

- After much thought, I felt that my responsibility was to tend to the home fires instead of saving the world with my software product.

Test the waters

The image of this phrase is one of a child putting his toe into water to see how cold it is. When you test the waters, you are trying to determine if something is worth your time or not?

Example:

- I need to test the waters to see if having my own business is something I want to do.

Textbook example

"Textbook examples" are classic situations or activities. It is spoken about in ideal situations. In other words, this is going exactly how the textbook said it would go. There are no deviations.

Example:

- This is a textbook example of how a transaction should occur.

Thanks but no cigar

This phrase is similar to "close but no cigar." It means "thanks for the offer, but I'll pass on it now."

Example:

- Tom asked me if I wanted to go with him to Madison. Thanks but no cigar.

That doesn't cut it

If "something doesn't cut it," it means that it is not up to standards. It doesn't mean that it is bad; it's just not great quality.

Example:

- You've only sold four boxes this week. Your quota is 10 boxes. That doesn't cut it.

That doesn't mean squat

This phrase simply means "that doesn't mean anything to me."

Example:

- If I were to tell you that there is a hurricane approaching Florida and I live in Alaska. That doesn't mean squat to me. It's a crude way to say, "so?"

That has a nice ring to it

Any phrase that sounds nice is said to have "a nice ring to

it." More specifically, this phrase is often used when you receive an award or degree that changes the title of your name, it sounds nice. It brings a smile to your face.

Example:

- Doctor Smith. Doctor Smith. Has a nice ring to it, doesn't it?

That project fell through

When a project "falls through," it has failed and does not reappear? This is related to "fall through the cracks."

Example:

- I recently interviewed for a job. The project manager got fired and so I was no longer needed for the position. The project that the manager was working on fell through as a result.

That separates the men from the boys

This phrase means that boys and men have different abilities. A task that separates the weak from the strong is separating the men from the boys.

Example:

- Climbing that mountain will certainly separate the men from the boys.

That struck a wrong chord

This means that something is not right about a person's situation of what he said. It may be deceptive but it just may be wrong.

Example:

- When he told me that he went around the world on his bike, it struck a wrong chord? I knew it couldn't be true.

That weighs a ton

This is simply an exaggeration or hyperbole. It is usually said about extremely heavy items.

Example:

- That textbook weighed a ton. It took me an hour to carry it up the stairs.

That's half the battle

Usually this is said when something easy is finished and there is a more difficult part remaining.

Example:

- In writing a book, writing the book is not even half the battle. Marketing is the other half.

That'll fly

This is another way of saying, "that'll work" or "I'm fine with that." This phrase is often used in the negative.

Example:

- Wait until I propose this project to the boss. Someone else reviews the same project and says, "Nope. It'll never fly."

That's all she wrote

This simply means "it's finished." If a piece of machinery dies, "it's all she wrote."

Example:

- When Simran got to know about her betrayed friend then that's all she wrote with her"

The city never sleeps

Cities tend to have a life of their own, especially at night. Small towns "sleep;" cities don't.

Example:

- When you wake in the middle of the night and wonder if a store is open to buy medicine, the city never sleeps.

The john

This is a crude way of saying the bathroom, restroom or toilet. Men say it.

Example:

- I need to go to the john.

The judge threw the book at him

If "the judge ever throws the book at you," you're in deep trouble. We usually say this when the judge issues a harsh penalty for a crime.

Example:

- He must have really angered the judge because the judge threw the book at him.

The last step's a dousey

Usually this phrase is used when someone nearly falls at the bottom of the stairs. They didn't see the last step.

Example:

- Whoops. That last step is a dousey (pronounced doo zee).

The little boys' room

This is a euphemism for the Men's bathroom or washroom. Normally, a person will say this when he is seated at a restaurant and there are women present. Women refer to their washroom as the "little girls' room."

Example:

- I need to run to the little boys' room. I'll be back in a second.

The man is king of his castle

When a man wants to let others know that he is the boss (usually at home but not always), he will say this?

Example:

- I am the king of this castle and what I say goes. Right, just don't forget to do the dishes.

The night is young

We would use this phrase when the person we took to the party wants to leave.

Example:

- Why do you want to leave so early; the night is still young?

The room was spotless

This phrase is similar to the previous phrase. "Spotless" implies no dirt or dust whatsoever.

Example:

- After the maid comes each week, their house is spotless.

Their marriage is on the rocks

If something is "on the rocks," it is shaky and needs something to help steady it. In other words, there are problems that need to be fixed in the marriage.

Example:

- After I went to Bermuda alone, my relationship with Jennifer was on the rocks.

There goes the neighbourhood

This phrase is often used in jest when a friend moves into your neighbourhood. It means that before he moved in everything about the neighbourhood was great. Now, we're not so sure.

Example:

- Tom and his family moved in next door. There goes the neighbourhood.

There's no love loss between them

If you hear this phrase (and you will because it is extremely popular), you can be certain that the two are strong competitors and probably enemies.

Example:

- When I saw Tom and Mary interact, I realise that after their split there really was no love loss between them?

They don't make them like they used to

This phrase is said when something common falls apart. There is a common notion that 40 or 50 years ago, things were made to last a long time. They were made of better materials and better craftsmanship.

Example:

- A new transmission after 50,000 miles? They sure don't make them like they used to.

This class is dead

"Dead" in this phrase means dull, boring, unlively. This applies to anything that is dull or boring.

Example:

- The comedian had a hard time because the audience was dead (unlively, bored).Freuency of usage: sometimes

This course is a joke

If a student tells you this, it does not mean that it is funny. It means that it is incredibly easy or a waste of time. It also applies to things that are very easy.

Example:

- I couldn't believe it. That seminar was a joke.

This has seen its day (old)

This expression usually refers to something that is old and worn. It is still useful but it looks old.

Example:

- Boy, that shirt has certainly seen its day. I bought that for you 10 years ago.

This hits home

When we hear news about tragic events, it rarely affects us. But when we hear that same news and hear that a local resident was involved, "it hits home?"

Example:

- 9/11 really hit home when I saw a photo of one of the hijackers. He lived right down the street from us!

This is a drag

This phrase means that something is boring or tedious and often undesirable.

Example:

- It was really a drag going to see my relatives' cousins.

This is gold (valuable)

Obviously gold is valuable. Information can also be gold. Usually this refers to a bit of information not previously known.

Example:

- When he told me that I was now a candidate for the Chairmanship that was gold?

This is shot

When something "is shot," it is unusable and worthless. Transmissions in cars, computers, anything can be shot?

Example:

- I examined the fax machine and it was totally shot.

Threw me for a loop

This is something, usually news that is totally unexpected.

Example:

- When he told me that he had been dating my sister for the last year, it threw me for a loop?

Throw caution into the wind

If you "throw caution into the wind," you are taking a huge risk. You are saying, "I know what I want and I also know what will happen if I fail, but I have to do it."

Example:

- He threw caution into the wind and took a year off work to travel around the world.

Throw his weight around

This phrase applies more to power than it does to physical weight. Someone who "throws their weight around" probably is close to abusing his power and authority. He is letting you know that he is the boss.

Example:

- He started to throw his weight around by telling us we couldn't take breaks.

Tickle the ivories

This simply means to play the piano. At one time piano keys were made of ivory.

Example:

- Would you help us out by tickling the ivories this morning for church?

Tie the knot

This phrase means to get married. We use it often.

Example:

- They finally decided to tie the knot.

Tightwad

A "tightwad" is someone who is very tight with his money. "Penny pincher" is a synonym. It is a derogatory term.

Example:

- He's such a tightwad. He won't even buy a single rose for his wife.

Time flies

The full expression is "time flies when you're having fun." It means that the hours go by quickly when you're enjoying yourself. In a broader sense, it can mean that the years go by quickly.

Example:

- Where did the time go today? Time sure flies.

To ace the test

When you "ace" something you get everything right?

Example:

- I was hoping to ace my exams, but got a B. I'm not happy about that.

To air dirty laundry

"To air dirty laundry" means to make private information public. Usually this information is negative and can damage reputations.

Example:

- Nobody likes dirty laundry, and yet everybody loves it (when it's not theirs).Frequency of usage: Sometimes

To ask Webster

"Webster" is a well-known publisher of dictionaries. When you "ask Webster," you are consulting a dictionary to research a dictionary.

Example:

- That's not what that word means. Let's talk to Mr. Webster about it.

To bark up the wrong tree

If you are "barking up the wrong tree" you are accusing someone of doing something that they didn't do. Or you're implying that somebody is responsible for action that he didn't do.

Example:

- The judge barked the wrong tree on the man.

To barrel down the road

This phrase means to drive down the road very quickly. It implies recklessness.

Example:

- We were barreling down the road until we saw the police car.

To be an animal

This phrase means many different things as it applies to humans. It can mean cruel, wild, or heinous. Context is important.

Example:

- What he did to those people, he's an animal.

To be behind/in front of the power curve

These phrases mean to be either late or early. The military uses it.

Example:

- Sorry folks, but we're behind the power curve a bit.

To be beside himself

A man who is "beside himself" is either very angry or extremely happy. This is even a confusing idiom for native speakers since the exact opposite emotions can be seen. Obviously context is very important.

Example:

- He was beside himself when he heard the news.

To be broke/busted

These two verbs mean to not have any money a tall. The next time you'll have money again is on payday.

Example:

- Sorry, I can't go with you to the game. I'm flat out broke.

To be burned

If a person "burns you," it may mean that he betrayed you.

Example:

- I loaned my friend money and she burned me. I haven't spoken to her in 3 years.

To be cold cocked

If you've been "cold cocked" you were hit hard unexpectedly.

Example:

- He was cold cocked before he knew what hit him.

To be floored

This phrase means "to be shocked" by the information or news.

Example:

- She floored me when she told me that I was boring.

To be had

This phrase means you were tricked or fooled.

Example:

- I found out that I had been had by the best in the business.

To be hard up

This phrase means that you are desperate or destitute. You need money to survive.

Example:

- After he lost his job, he was hard up for work.

To be hooked

If you are hooked on something, it means that you cannot live without it. You are addicted to it. Drugs, tobacco, alcohol are all things you can be hooked on.

Example:

- It only takes a few snorts of cocaine to be hooked on drugs.

To be loaded

This phrase can mean that a person is carrying a lot of money or is worth a lot of money.

Example:

- Look at that new car! He must be loaded.

To be old hat

A person who is very good at doing one particular thing is "old hat."

Example:

- He's an old hat when building houses. He can do it in his sleep.

To be on his soapbox again

When a person has strong political opinions and voices them, he is on his soapbox?

Example:

- I wish he'd get off his soapbox.

To be out cold

A person who is "out cold" is unconscious. Quite possibly he is asleep and shaking him won't wake him.

Example:

- After George's head hit the pillow, he was out cold.

To be plastered

This phrase means to get really drunk.

Example:

- He didn't remember much about last night because he was plastered.

To be pretty rank

You stink if you are "pretty rank." It simply means that

something stinks. Normally this doesn't apply to people but it can.

Example:

- I took out the garbage because it was getting pretty rank.

To be railroaded

If you've ever been "railroaded," you know what it's like to be falsely accused with very little evidence.

Example:

- To save his daughter from jail, he was railroaded into confessing crimes he didn't commit.

To be really wired

This phrase can mean two different things: (1) a person is very energetic and excited or (2) a person is drunk.

Example:

- When he found out the test results, he was really wired?

To be stoned

If you are "stoned," you are drunk or high on drugs.

Example:

- He came to the party already half-stoned.

To be stood up

This phrase generally applies to dating but I've heard it elsewhere. If you are "stood up" on a date, it means that you planned on meeting a person but the person never came.

Example:

- I can't believe he stood me up. What is his problem?

To be stuffed

This means something different in England, but since these are American idioms, it means to be full with food. You cannot eat anything else.

Example:

- After that meal, I was completely stuffed. I went home and took a nap.

To bend over backwards

Normally you "bend over backwards" to help someone. It means you do what it takes and sacrifice to help.

Example:

- I bent over backwards to help him and THIS is what he did to me!

To biff it

This is a slang way that means to "blow it" or to fail as a result of your actions.

Example:

- I biffed it this time. I was supposed to go to the meeting but I didn't want to go.

To blow it

This phrase means to fail as a result of your actions.

Example:

- I really blew it this time. I didn't study hard enough for the test.Frequency of usage: Often

To blow it off

If you "blow something off," you intentionally ignore it.

Example:

- I blew off the test because I hadn't even studied for it. I was failing anyhow.

To breathe fire

If someone is "breathing fire," he is ready to release anger or has already done so. He is extremely angry.

Example:

- Watch out! The boss is breathing fire today.

To burn out

"To burn out" means to be weary and tired of doing something over and over again. People working in "people" professions burnout quickly: psychologists, pastors, counselors, etc.

Example:

- He needs a long vacation or else he'll burn out.

To buy into

If you "buy into" an idea, for instance, you are not paying any money, but you are beginning to accept the idea. Before this, you might have been opposed to the idea.

Example:

- It took a long time but I think he's now buying into the idea.

To cheer someone on

This phrase implies that fans or supporters are surrounding an athlete and through their shouts and cheers are helping them to finish the race. It is a general term for encouragement.

Example:

- We came to the race to cheer Anne on.

To chip in

When you "chip in" for something, you are one of many who will pay for an item. It is to share the cost or workload. You will also all share the item.

Example:

- Let's all chip in for some pizza.

To chow down

This phrase means to eat quickly, often sloppily. It is a male term. Women would not use this phrase usually.

Example:

- Let's chow down before the food gets cold.

To clean house

The idea behind this idiom is simple. It means that we're going to win everything.

Example:

- We are about to clean the house in this competition.

To crack down

The very broad definition of this phrase is to enforce something that already exists.

Example:

- Mr. Suresh cracked down on his kids: curfew was now at 9 p:m for the rest of the school year.

To crash on the bed

Sometimes after a long day at work you just want to go home and "crash." It simply means to lay down and probably go to sleep. It implies that you do nothing else except rest.

Example:

- I went home and crashed after work last night.

To cut down someone

To "cut someone down" means to insult him.

Example:

- He cut me down because I wore shorts in the winter.

To cut out (let's go)

This phrase simply means to go or to leave.

Example:

- Let's cut out of here and go to a restaurant.

To cut up (joke)

If you are accused of "cutting up" a lot, you are probably a funny person. This phrase means to joke and to "poke fun" at others. This use of the phrase is not mean or cruel.

Example:

- Everyone seemed to be cutting up at the party.

To die down

If something "dies down," it slows down or decreases.

Example:

- After the noise died down a bit, the speaker spoke.

To die out

Usually this means a slow death to either machinery or a movement. It implies a "death" little by little.

Example:

- The push to impeach the president is dying out.

To do it up right

Parties and major events are "done up right." Usually they are well decorated, have plenty of food and drinks, and are well attended. The phrase is very slang and informal.

Example:

- The Jenny's really know how to do their house up right for Christmas.

To do or die

This is it. Either this works or we are completely finished

(it rarely means death). We also refer to "do or die" situations.

Example:

- He needed to get a C on this test to pass the course. For him it was do or die.

To do time

If you have "done time," you have been in jail. It can also be a joke to mean working at an undesirable business.

Example:

- He did time in three different states. Did he work in 3 states or was he in jail in 3 states. Without context we don't know.

To draw a blank

Simply, it means that you forgot something you should have known, perhaps a name or telephone number.

Example:

- Help me out. I'm drawing a blank.

To draw a line in the sand

Someone "draws a line in the sand" to set up a challenge or warning. The implication is this: If you cross this line you'll be in trouble.

Example:

- I've drawn the line; don't cross it. If you do, there will be a big price to pay.

To draw the line

Everyone has limits to what he can or can't do. Everybody has to draw a line to establish those limits. The limits are different for each person.

Example:

- You have to draw the line somewhere lest people walk all over you.

To drive a point home

You have a point or an idea you are trying to present. In order for that idea to stick in a person's mind, you "drive the point home" with an illustration or example that the person will remember. You make the idea memorable.

Example:

- He drove the point home with a personal illustration.

To drop a line

"Drop a line" means to write a letter. Usually it is used in written form at the end of a letter. You want the other person to "drop a line when you get a chance." The letter writer is hoping for even a short three or four lines "just to say hi" and that "I'm thinking about you.

Example:

- Drop a line. I'd love to hear from you.

To drum up more business

When your business is not doing well, the manager might suggest you think of new ways to "drum up more business?" Perhaps you'll place more ads, make some phone calls, or pass out business cards. All of these are ways to increase business and make more sales.

Example:

- Get out there on the streets and drum up more business.

To each his own

This means that each person has his own tastes, desires, values, beliefs.

Example:

- When I see a person with strange hair colors or styles, I may shake my head and say to myself, "to each his own?"

To earn your keep

If you are staying as a guest in someone's house for a few days, you may jokingly ask what you can do to earn your keep.

Example:

- If I'm staying here for two weeks I want to earn my keep.

To face the music

Nobody likes to "face the music." "The music" here is consequences for your actions.

Example:

- The four students played a great joke on the principal. Now they must face the music.

To fall in love

Usually this phrase implies a quick "love at first sight" encounter. Falling in love is getting to know the person, their likes, dislikes values, views and everything about them. It is rarely "love at first sight." Many English songs are about "falling in love."

Example:

- I fell in love with her last year and am still in love.

To fall into a trap

Usually this phrase relates to thinking. A trap is something that hunters use to catch animals. When the animal falls in, it cannot climb out. Falling into a trap means that after you begin thinking one way it is difficult to think another way.

Example:

- Before Sam was fired, he had fallen into the trap of thinking that he was indispensable to the company.

To fill their shoes

When a person moves away, he leaves a void at a company? The job of the company is to "fill that person's shoes." The new person must do as much as the previous person and still maintain his own personality.

Example:

- When Barry left, there were some very big shoes to fill at work?

To fit the description to a tee

If the police are searching for a tall white man, aged 30, red shirt, jeans, purple shoes and a scar on the left side of his face, and you happen to have all of those features; you "fit the description to a tee." Somebody is looking for you.

Example:

- I didn't realise that you fit the description to a tee until I saw the purple shoes.

To flag someone down

If you "flag someone down," you are by the roadside and your car is broken down. You wave for a person to stop.

Example:

- We tried to flag down the first car that came but it soared right past us.

To gear up for

When you "gear up for something" you are either physically or mentally preparing to do it. In the broadest sense it is taking steps to prepare yourself.

Example:

- Everyone around here is gearing up for Winter.

To get a jump on it

We would also say this is "getting a head start." Picture in your mind runners at the beginning of a race. In a short race, it is critical to get a good start, even if only by a fraction of a second. This is the idea of getting a jump.

Example:

- I need to get a jump on this term paper before I forget about it completely.

To get hung up on that

If you are "hung up on something," you cannot move past it. When you are speaking, you can be "hung up" on an idea?

Example:

- When we started talking about baseball, he got hung up on the multi-million dollar salaries. He just couldn't get beyond it. We even tried to talk about politics but he was still hung up on the wealthy ball players.

To get in gear

If someone says to you, "get it in gear," it either means to go faster or to start moving.

Example:

- We're running late. Get it into gear, okay?

To get on the stick

"Get on the stick" is similar to "get it into gear." It has the idea of going from a slow pace to a faster pace. You are not in a big hurry, but you want to move faster.

Example:

- Michael was taking his time getting ready for school until I told him to get on the stick.

To get roped into

This is a humorous phrase that implies that I really do not want to be involved in this. Someone convinces you to do something you don't really want to do.

Example:

- One person is volunteering to help another to fix his car. He thought the project would take 10 minutes. After an hour the project is only half completed. He then asks, "how'd you ever rope me into this?"

To get shafted

If you ever "get shafted," you were probably upset about it. It means that somebody intentionally tricked you and you lost money as a result. However, if you "got the shaft," it means that you got fired from your job.

Example:

- I got the shaft after I showed up for work late every day last week.

To get snookered

This phrase means two things depending on the context. *First*, it means to be fooled into doing something, usually with a loss of money.

Example:

- He got snookered into buying the most expensive tennis racket.

To go to the can

This phrase is similar to "the john." It is the bathroom,

washroom, restroom, and toilet. It is less crude than the john but still very informal. Men will use this phrase more often than women.

Example:

- I need to go to the can, man.

To go to town!

If someone "really goes to town" they do something really quickly. Context is important.

Example:

- Did you see those workers eat! Man, they were really going to town.

To goof up

This means to make mistakes. These generally are honest mistakes and not intentional. Sometimes it is used without the preposition "up."

Example:

- Sorry, I goofed up. I gave his tickets to her.

To have a hankering for

"A hankering" is a strong desire for, a yearning for something you've enjoyed before.

Example:

- She had a hankering for a Caesar Salad at the River Front Café.

To have a lot of pull

If you "have a lot of pull," you are "connected" and may have power "to make things happen." Politicians tend to have a lot of pull. If you have pull, you can make a phone call or two to help someone get a job.

Example:

- I'm not worried. My husband has a lot of pull at his company. He's a vice president there.

To have clout

"Clout" and "pull" as mentioned above is very similar. If you have clout, you have high standing and therefore have a lot of authority or pull (a lot of respect or influence).

Example:

- Jane has a lot of clout in the industry. When she speaks at a conference, people listen very carefully.

To have him wrapped around her finger

This phrase generally applies to women and children. It means they have power over the man. She tells him that he can't go out and he doesn't.

Example:

- One of these days Hank will stand up to his wife. Until then, though, she has him wrapped around her little finger.

To have his act together

You want to be around a person who has his act together. He is prepared and alert, sharp and intelligent, funny and honest. He doesn't criticise. In general, a person who has his act together is a person of noble character.

Example:

- Why can't you learn from Larry? He's really got his act together.

To hit paydirt

This is a phrase we occasionally use to mean "we struck it rich." It has its origins when people mined for gold. Paydirt is earth that yields profit. This phrase means that you've discovered a valuable source of riches, *i.e.*, information, data, etc.

Example:

- We searched for a full 2 hours; then we hit paydirt, the information we needed was all there in one file.

To hit the hay/rack/sack

All three words hay, rack, and sack mean the same thing when you hit it. It means you went to bed.

Example:

- We were exhausted so we hit the sack.

To hit the road

When you "hit the road," you are leaving? When you tell someone to "hit the road," you are telling them to leave?

Example:

- We were not welcome there anymore so we hit the road.

To jump on the bandwagon

A bandwagon is any new trend or fashion or idea or sports team that most of society has already embraced. The problem with bandwagons in today's society is that it changes so often.

Example:

- The newest trend in software is e-commerce. Our company has finally accepted the idea and has jumped on the bandwagon.

To jump to conclusions

When you "jump to a conclusion" you have judged an idea before someone explained it fully?

Example:

- Hear me out before you jump to any conclusions. What I have to say in the end may prevent you from jumping ahead?

To keep his cool

This simply means "to keep calm" despite chaotic surroundings or something that would normally anger or excite an average person.

Example:

- When the fire started, he kept his cool and helped others out the door?

To keep them guessing

If you "keep people guessing," you are probably

unpredictable. If people think you'll respond by saying X, you'll say Y. You are unpredictable.

Example:

- I like to keep people guessing about me. It makes life so enjoyable.

To keep them hopping

If, on the other hand, you "keep them hopping," you are keeping them busy. They don't have time to think and complain about all the work while they are working.

Example:

- I think if you want this division to be productive, you have to keep them hopping.

To lay it on thick

This phrase means that the person talking is probably lying or "stretching the truth." It is also possible that the person is excessively flattering somebody else. We would say that the person is "laying it on thick."

Example:

- When someone lays it on thick, I let them know it?

To line his pockets

"You line your pockets" generally with money. You are the head of an organisation and somebody give you a lot of money. When you take money that was intended for the organisation that is lining your pockets?

Example:

- It's easy to see how he's so rich. With every deal that came alone, he was lining his pockets.

To live life fat, dumb and happy

These three adjectives are used together often. Essentially it means that you have no cares, are content and don't know what's happening around you. Some people would even prefer to live that way!

Example:

- If I'm living fat, dumb and happy, all is well with me.

To look spiffy

If you are "looking spiffy," you are very well dressed for the occasion. Places and events can also look spiffy if they are well decorated.

Example:

- I must say, he was looking very spiffy for a mechanic.

To lose his touch

Generally this phrase is used about a person who is very skilled but for whatever reason is losing that skill. It is often used jokingly.

Example:

- Five years ago Al could get a date in a bar in 10 minutes. Now it takes him a half hour. He must be losing his touch.

To lose it

This phrase means "to become angry" or to lose control of emotions (cry). It implies that he was no longer in control of his emotions.

Example:

- He saw that photo of his ex-girlfriend and lost it completely.

To lose sleep over it

This expression is usually used in the negative. If you're told "not to lose sleep over it," it means you shouldn't worry about it because it is probably small. I have also heard it in reference to another person. The person is "not losing any sleep over her," probably because he has another girl or a lot of time has passed.

Example:

- It was only five dollars that was stolen. I wouldn't lose sleep over it.

To love the limelight

"Limelight" is attention. You want to be noticed. You enjoy the attention. Perhaps TV cameras and microphones are involved, but not always. You just like being put into the spotlight.

Example:

- That lady was born to be a star. She loves the limelight.

To make beaucoup bucks

Simply, if someone is making "beaucoup bucks,"

(pronounced bo koo or boo koo) he is earning a lot of money.

Example:

- Would you look at that guy? He must be raking in beaucoup bucks.

To make ends meet

If you are able to "make ends meet," you have just enough income to pay all your bills. It is a very common phrase, especially in the lower middle class of America.

Example:

- He had just enough money this month to make ends meet. Next month he might not be as fortunate.

To make the grade

This phrase means "to be good enough." It is a standard that must be met.

Example:

- She needs to be able to lift 75 pounds (32 kilograms) to make the grade at the fire station.

To manhandle

If you are "manhandled," you have been "pushed around" by others, either physically or otherwise. You weren't in a fight. You were just pushed around.

Example:

- After my speech, a few protestors manhandled my supporters.

To moonlight

To "moonlight" is to have a second or third job in order to have money to "make ends meet."

Example:

- After he bought the second car he had to moonlight for a few months to help pay for it.

To mull over

This phrase means to "think about" something.

Example:

- He's mulling over the option of working overtime.

To nickel and dime it

If you buy an inexpensive product, you don't need the salesman "to nickel and dime" it so that it's even more expensive.

Example:

- I wish there was a law that prevented salesmen from nickling and diming you after the sale.

To open up

This essentially means to express yourself, to "bare" your true inner emotions and feelings, to say what's on your mind.

Example:

- Women, as a rule, tend to open up better and more easily than men.

To pack it up

"To pack it up" means to get ready to leave or go. It has a sense of completion.

Example:

- You are on a construction project and it's 5 p.m. If you pack it up, you'll gather your tools, lunchbox and load up your truck. You'll tell your co-workers "good bye" and go home. You packed it up for the day.

To panhandle

"To panhandle" means to beg for money. A person who panhandles is a panhandler.

Example:

- Recently the City issued a new law stating that panhandling is not permitted during normal business hours.

To pay under the table

If you are "paying under the table," you are probably helping a person to avoid paying taxes. You are intentionally trying to hide the fact that you are paying in cash (or that the company is accepting it in cash).

Example:

- If you pay under the table, nobody will ever have to know. You will, however, have to live with your own conscience.

To pitch in

This simply means to help. It can also mean to share or to

chip in financially.

Example:

- The Boy Scouts saw us by the road, stopped, and pitched in to help change our tire.

To play up to the boss

It means that you'll approach the boss to let him know that if he needs any additional help, you will do it. It is getting into the boss' good favor.

Example:

- I heard it with my own ears. Vijay was intentionally playing up to the boss when I passed them in the hall.

To play with fire

This is the full expression: if you play with fire, you will get burned. Or if you "mess with fire you'll get burned." Beyond the obvious explanation is a more subtle meaning.

Example:

- Regarding drugs, if you play with fire (drugs) you will get burned (addicted, jail, etc.).

To press the issue

This phrase has the idea that you are trying to "force" an issue. You want a decision so you keep bringing it up. You won't let the issue drop. You are trying to prove your point.

Example:

- He pressed the issue one too many times so I told him I didn't want to talk about it.

To pull it off

This phrase means "to make it happen," despite odds that it might not happen. If something you plan goes wrong in the middle but comes out fine in the end, you have pulled it off.

Example:

- I don't know how they did it, but somehow they managed to pull it off at the last minute.

To raise Cain

"Raising Cain" can mean someone who causes trouble or someone who voices concerns and complaints about something.

Example:

- At the party last night, they raised a lot of Cain.

To raise the roof

If you "raise the roof" you are angry and are yelling. You were upset about something and voiced your outrage.

Example:

- When Adam found out about the lost revenue, he raised the roof at our next meeting?

To reach a happy medium

If you "reach a happy medium," you are probably negotiating. The happy medium is the middle ground.

Example:

- Your buyer wants to pay 50 rupees for the product.

You want to sell it for 100 rupees. The happy medium is 75 rupees and both of you are satisfied.

To red-line it

This phrase can have two distinct meanings depending on context. The first is to edit something.

Example:

- You have determined that the project will not work so you red-line it.

To roast him

Typically when a person is honoured bynhis co-workers, he is the center of attention at a large banquet. Friends and relatives will "roast" him by making him the "butt" of all jokes. In the end, they present a great award for his achievements. It's light-hearted and all in fun.

Example:

- They were roasting Bill at the Awards Ceremony but he wasn't laughing hard.

To save the day

If you have ever "saved the day," you were probably in good favor with many people. It means that you found a solution to a problem that nobody had known about. You solved the problem when no one else could. You are, in essence, the hero for the day.

Example:

- I'm not sure exactly what I did to save the day, but I'll accept it.

To saw logs

Someone who "saw logs," especially at night, snores loudly.

Example:

- I tried to get some sleep last night but somebody was sawing logs all night.

To scale a tree

If you can "scale a tree," it means you can climb it quickly. This applies to walls, mountains and anything else that is difficult to climb.

Example:

- When the dog was chasing the cat, the cat scaled the tree in record time?

To slack off

You don't ever want to be accused of "slacking off" on the job. It means that your production is lower than normal. It is also used in jest occasionally.

Example:

- Normally he makes 1000 widgets a day. Today he only 750. He must be slacking off.

To slough off

"To slough off" means to ignore or "blow off" an assignment. For whatever reason, you don't want to do it. It can also mean to pass the assignment to someone else. It's usually an assignment that no one wanted to do.

Example:

- I was so angry at Matt. He got that job but sloughed it off to me, then laughed while I was doing it.

To smell victory

Obviously, you cannot smell victory physically. Nor can you taste it or feel it but we use all three of those senses when it comes to victory. It is within our grasp. We only need to finish it.

Example:

- Only one more play left in the game and we could all smell victory.

To spin his wheels

If you "spin your wheels" on ice or snow, you are not going anywhere. Similarly, if you spin your wheels doing something, you're wasting your time and not going anywhere.

Example:

- If I were you, I wouldn't date her. She's married. You're just spinning your wheels.

To sponge off of

We might also use the verb "to mooch." If I let you stay in my house for a year and you don't pay for rent, food or bills, you are sponging off me.

Example:

- Nate was sponging off us for more than a month. Then I told him to go find a job.

To spruce it up a bit

This simply means to clean it up. Women will spruce up a bit in restaurants. That is, they will go to the washroom to reapply makeup, lipstick, comb their hair.

Example:

- Excuse us while we go spruce up a bit.

To square off

If you are "squaring off" with someone, you are in direct competition with them, typically face-to-face or one to one.

Example:

- The racers were squaring off for the first time ever man to man, head to head.

To stay put

This phrase means to remain where you are. Don't move until someone tells you otherwise.

Example:

- After they had moved all throughout the singing, I told them to stay put during the preaching.

To stick around

"Stick around" means to stay. It is related to "hang around."

Example:

- The main event is starting. Are you sticking around?

To stop on a dime

This means to stop abruptly.

Example:

- That car has excellent brakes. It can stop on a dime.

To string us along

If a person "strings you along," he is promising you things and then one day he disappears. It has the idea of being led into a trap and then that trap ensnares you.

Example:

- For a full month, he had been stringing us along, telling us that he would go with us to Shimla, then he backed out.

To sweat bullets

If you are sweating bullets, you are very nervous. Sweat is pouring from your face.

Example:

- He was sweating bullets until he found out the results from the doctor.

To sweep under the rug

When you hide dirt under a rug, the dirt is still there. It's just not visible. This expression means that a project or plan was an embarrassment and people wanted to hide it so they "forgot about it." Actually, the people probably didn't want to deal with it.

Example:

- Be careful that the project just doesn't get swept under the rug with Jim as manager. He tends to forget things he doesn't like.

To take the heat

This phrase refers to someone who personally will take responsibility for a group's actions.

Example:

- When the boss asked who was responsible for the accounting error, Ted spoke up and said it was him, even though we all knew that we had a part in it? He was willing to take the heat for us.

To the tune of ...

Usually this means "to the sum of..." but it deals with large sums of money and often with regret.

Example:

- We bought a motor home last month, to the tune of 55,000.Frequency of usage:Sometimes

To throw a party

When you "throw a party," you are merely hosting it.

Example:

- Beth threw a party last week.

To thumb a ride

We call this "hitchhiking." In rural areas, it's a lot more popular. It was extremely popular in the 60s and 70s.

Basically, you stand alongside the road and put your thumb out. Drivers then know you need a ride. If they think you are trustworthy, they will pick you up and take you as far as they are going.

Example:

- As a last resort, I'll thumb a ride from someone.

To tighten our belt

If you "tighten your belt," you are carefully monitoring your spending.

Example:

- We barely have enough money at the end of the month. We'll need to tighten our belt a little more.

To tighten the screws

If you are "tightening the screws," it means you are applying pressure or tightening standards.

Example:

- He's been coming home later and later. I think I need to tighten some screws.

To tip the bottle

If you "tip the bottle," you drink alcohol. The term generally applies to somebody who has been drinking.

Example:

- Just ignore what he says tonight. He's been tipping the bottle.

To toe the line

If you are asked to "toe the line," one of two things could be happening. *First*, a police officer asks you to toe the line to see if you can walk in a straight line. It is one of the tests to determine if you are too drunk to drive. *Secondly*, a more popular usage means to adhere to the rules.

Example:

- You'd better start toeing the line, young man.

Tough pill to swallow

A "tough pill to swallow" is usually very bad news. The person will have a difficult time digesting the information. This phrase is typically about bad news and rarely is about medicine.

Example:

- He says he likes Katrina, my best friend. Wow! That's a tough pill to swallow.

To weed out

This phrase generally means to filter through the good and bad, and throw out the bad.

Example:

- Early in training, the Army tries to weed out those who cannot obey the rules.

To wise up

This verb simply means to behave more. Parents usually use this with their children.

Example:

- You'd better wise up if you want to go to the concert this weekend.

Tone down

If you "tone it down," you are trying to reduce the noise level or you are trying to soften harsh words.

Example:

- Hey, hey, tone it down in here. I'm trying to concentrate.

Toot your own horn

This refers to a person who is boasting about his own skills and accomplishments.

Example:

- Tony said, "I don't want to toot my own horn but I did write a skit for just that occasion."

Top notch

Someone who is top notch is excellent. He is skilled, trustworthy, and first class. You want to associate with a top notch person or organization.

Example:

- You said the organization moved you to a new location and paid for everything? That's a top notch group.

Toss and turn all night

A person cannot sleep if she "tosses and turns all night."

She has been turning around on the bed trying to get to sleep.

Example:

- I didn't sleep a wink last night. I was tossing and turning all night.

Toy around with

This phrase is similar to "to play around with" or "to monkey with." We also call it "trial and error." It means that a solution is not obvious so you must try various methods to fix something. It has the idea of play in order to get something to work.

Example:

- I toyed around with the computer for an hour until I got it right.

Tread on thin ice

This phrase indicates that a subject is delicate and should be treated gently. In other words, don't go too much further in the conversation or you'll be in trouble.

Example:

- Watch it, Pal! You're treading on thin ice when you bring up hunting and fishing with this group.

Trip the light fantastic

If you trip the light fantastic, you are dancing. It was a lot more common 30 years ago.

Example:

- You should have seen me last night. I tripped the light fantastic!

Trouble is his middle name

Any time that you hear a word such as trouble or fun or genius or brainy or muscles as a middle name, it means that word can be associated with the person. In the idiom it means that you need to be careful of this person because anywhere he goes, it means trouble.

Example:

- Stay clear of Salim. Trouble's his middle name.

Turn in for the night

This means that you are preparing to go to bed. You may not actually go to sleep but you are headed that way.

Example:

- After the poker game, we decided that we needed to turn in for the night so that we could get up early the next morning to go hunting.

Turn out the lights; the party's over

When something is finished, you will often hear this. It is officially time to go home.

Example:

- After a fight broke out, we decided it was time to turn out the lights because the party was definitely over.

Turn over a new leaf

"A new leaf" is a new beginning. Usually this refers to someone, possibly a criminal, is making progress towards reforming his behavior. He is beginning over again and making sure he doesn't get into trouble.

Example:

- You'd never know that he was in jail for 7 years. He's certainly turned over a new leaf.

Turn the tide

If "the tide" is going with you, you will sail out to sea. If it is against you, you won't go anywhere (and often backwards). Therefore, the tide is turning, it means things are looking more positive for you. Things are starting to go your way.

Example:

- The organisation is huge, but somehow I need to turn the tide so that they'll start thinking my way.

Turn up the heat

To "turn up the heat," means to put more pressure to do something. You can turn up the heat in projects, politics, and relationships.

Example:

- I need to know if he's committed to me or not. I'll have to turn up the heat a bit.

Two sheets to the wind

This phrase is another way of saying a person is drunk. I have also heard it as "three sheets to the wind."

Example:

- Don't ask him; he's two sheets to the wind and won't be sober for another day.

Two sides to a coin

If you only hear one side of a story, you're only hearing half of it. All stories have at least two sides, probably more. If, after hearing a version of a story, you think you need to hear the other side, you may use this phrase. The other person's version of the exact same story may be very different.

Example:

- Mary told me that Ron wasn't treating her well. Since there are two sides to a coin, I wanted to hear Ron's version.

Under the gun

If you are "under the gun," you are under pressure to get something done in a specified time.

Example:

- I wish I could have done a better job, but I was under the gun. The manager "turned up the heat" on me.

Under the weather

You are not feeling well if you are "under the weather."

Example:

- I was under the weather so I took a day off work.

Up and at 'em

A parent, drill sergeant or roommate will use this to tell you that it's time to get up. It literally means, "wake up and get out of bed." Normally the person saying this has been up for a while.

Example:

- Rise and shine! Up and at 'em.

Up to snuff

This phrase is identical to the next idiom. It means "up to standards."

Example:

- If this isn't up to snuff in a week, we'll cancel the project.

Up to speed

This phrase is identical to the previous idiom. It means "up to standards." This idiom has an additional meaning. It means to be "brought up to date."

Example:

- Let me bring you up to speed on what's been happening here lately.

Use every word in the book

A person who "uses every word in the book" is very angry. This is a reference to using all known profanity.

Example:

- You have obviously done something to anger this person if he uses every word in the book.

Wait with bated breath

This phrase means that you were waiting anxiously. It is highly anticipated. This can be a slightly sarcastic remark. Probably the only time you will see this in writing is in this e-book. It is a spoken comment.

Example:

- We'll be waiting with bated breath for his first novel to come out.

Waiting in the wings

Someone who is "waiting in the wings" is next in line to lead or take someone's place. He is learning all he can about leading, probably from observing the current leader.

Example:

- Sonam is waiting in the wings, biding his time until Don't step down.

Wake up and smell the roses

This is an extremely popular phrase. This simply means to become aware of what is happening around you. It has another variation that is also popular: Wake up and smell the coffee.

Example:

- Raja is dead. Wake up and smell the roses!

Walking time bomb

A person is considered a "walking time bomb" if he has many ailments and diseases. Typically the person is obese and doesn't watch what he eats.

Example:

- Look at the way he's eating all of the fatty food. He's a walking time bomb.

Walk a mile in his shoes

This phrase is used to avert undue criticism of someone. In order to fully understand a person, you must first "walk in his shoes," to know what he has gone through. The implication is that after you walk in his shoes, your view of him will change.

Example:

- Walk a mile in his shoes before you say anything bad about him.

Walk down memory lane

"Memory lane" is a place all of us go occasionally. It's our memories. Hence, when we "walk down memory lane" we are thinking about fond memories.

Example:

- I walked down memory lane recently with a good friend. We laughed and cried the entire night.

Walk the aisle

"Walk the aisle" is a euphemism for getting married.

Example:

- It's been 20 long years since I walked the aisle.

Wall to wall people

If you have "wall to wall" anything, there is a lot of it. Wall to wall carpeting is very common in America and this is where the term originates.

Example:

- I could barely move at that party. There were wall to wall people.

Watch your language

When a man is using harsh or coarse language, usually around women and children, someone may tell him to "watch his language." In other words, be careful what you say.

Example:

- When he told dirty jokes around the ladies, I told him to watch his language?

Water under the bridge

This is a phrase that means "let's not worry about that anymore. It's history." The water has passed and we can no longer do anything about it. Let's move on.

Example:

- I can't believe I loaned him money and he left town. Oh well, that's water under the bridge.

We bailed him out

When you "bail someone out," you are helping someone in trouble? You are getting them out of a bad situation.

Example:

- I'm really grateful to him. He bailed me out when the project was shaky.

We cracked up

This phrase generally means to laugh really hard.

Example:

- I can't believe he said that. We cracked up so hard there were tears in our eyes.

We got slaughtered

This phrase means that we lost, typically a competition, big. We weren't even close to winning.

Example:

- Truman High School slaughtered Fairmont High 49-0. It wasn't pretty.

We stand behind our work

This expression means that we are proud of our work and will guarantee that you will be satisfied with it. We did the work and will redo it if we need to.

Example:

- They had a money-back guarantee. If we weren't satisfied, we'd get our money back. They stand behind what they do.

Wear a plastic smile

A "plastic smile" is a fake smile.

Example:

- Look at that photo. That smile is just so plastic.

Wear his Sunday best

If someone is "wearing his Sunday best," it means he is dressed up for the occasion. In the previous century, everyone dressed upon Sundays. It was distinct from weekday attire.

Example:

- How could anything possibly go wrong? He was wearing his Sunday best.

Wear many hats

A person who "wears many hats" has many responsibilities and jobs. We all wear many hats. Normally this applies to a person in a company. He is manager, programmer, supervisor, and hiring person.

Example:

- I am a husband, a son, a teacher, a lecturer, an uncle, a writer, and a businessman. I wear many hats.

Wear out his welcome

If you visit a friend for 2-3 days you're a guest. If you stay for a week, 2 weeks, or a month, you are no longer a guest.

Example:

- You are "wearing out your welcome." They've grown tired of you.

Well rounded

Someone who is "well-rounded" is very good in many things. For instance, if he is a good salesman, marketer, manager and co-worker, he is considered well rounded.

Example:

- Well rounded teens are hard to find.

We're in business

This phrase means that "we are ready to move forward because everything is in line." It can be as simple as connecting electrical wires to constructing an entire building. A similar idiom is "we're good to go."

Example:

- Just one more decoration on the tree and we're in business.

Were you born in a barn?

You will hear this phrase when a door to a house or a car is left open. It's a question that really means, "shut the door."

Example:

- When I got in the car, my mother shouted from the house, "were you born in a barn?" I went back to shut the door.

What a doll

This is one of the many ways that men describe women. If a woman is a doll, she is gorgeous and very desirable.

Example:

- She's a doll. Too bad she's already taken.

What goes around comes around

You might hear this when someone has been hurt or offended. It means that the wrong that was done to me will be done to that person eventually. It's not a threat or revenge, merely an observation of life. Unfortunately, or fortunately depending on how you view it, life doesn't always work that way.

Example:

- I can't believe he did that. What goes around comes around.

What I don't know won't hurt me

This is a naive observation people make but you'll hear it quite often. It means that "if I close my eyes and I don't know what is happening around me, it can't affect me." It is especially used in the second person.

Example:

- He's been having an affair with a married woman. What his wife doesn't know won't hurt her.

What in the world?

This is identical to the previous question. If you took out "in the world" it would have the same meaning.

Example:

- What in the world are you doing with that knife?

What makes him tick?

This can be loosely translated as, "why does he do what he does?" What motivates him?

Example:

- I have no idea what makes that kid tick.

What of it?

This is a response to a mild challenge. It can be translated as "what are you going to do about it?" A person feels threatened.

Example:

- I wrote this. What of it?

What's going down?

This is exactly the same as "what's going on?" or "what's happening?"

Example:

- I saw all the cop cars. What's going down?

What's shaking?

This phrase means the same as "what's happening? or "how are you?"

Example:

- Hey, long time no see. What's shaking?

What's the big idea?

This question can be paraphrased like this: What happened here? Why was this done like this?

Example:

- I felt somebody hit me from behind so I turned around and asked, "hey, what's the big idea?"

What's the holdup?

The literal meaning of the word "holdup" is a robbery. But this phrase actually means, why are you taking so long? What's the delay?

Example:

- We've been waiting for an hour. What's the holdup?

What's the scoop?

A "scoop" is news that no one has printed yet. You have the exclusive news. When you ask, "what's the scoop?" it can be translated, "what's the news?" Sometimes it can mean simply, "how are you?"

Example:

- I saw the ambulance nearby. What's the scoop?

What's the word?

This phrase is a typical greeting along the lines of "how are you?" and "what's new?"

Example:

- Good to see you again. What's the word?

What's up?

Without question this is probably the most well-known and used greeting. It is probably bigger than "how are you?"

Example:

- How are you doing? What's up?

Where's the fire?

This phrase means "What's the rush?" and "What's the hurry?"

Example:

- Slow down. Where's the fire?

Who charged his battery?

It means that a person is energetic or excited. Who or what caused this person to become so energetic or excited? This particular questions deals with someone who is excited or very energetic.

Example:

- That kid just will not stop. Who charged his battery this morning?

Whole ball of wax

The next two phrases are identical in meaning. They simply mean everything available.

Example:

- I told him to come prepared for the camping trip. He brought the whole ball of wax.

Whole kit and caboodle

This phrase is identical to "the whole ball of wax."

Example:

- They brought the whole kit and caboodle on the trip with them. You name it; they brought it.

Who lit his candle?

It is similar to who or what caused this person to become so angry or excited.

Example:

- Who lit his candle? Stay away from him, is all I can say?

Who tripped his trigger?

Usually this question is asked about a person who is angry and overexcited. Who or what caused this person to become so angry or excited?

Example:

- Who tripped Tim's trigger today? He wasn't like that last night.

Who will chair that committee?

To chair a committee means to lead it. He or she is responsible for setting the meeting agendas and activities.

Example:

- If Dr. Rajan chairs that committee, I'm glad to join the company.

Who wound him up?

If I see a person who is behaving abnormally, either good or bad, I may ask this question. We might also say it if a person is angry or excited or very energetic. In other words, what caused this person to become so lively?

Example:

- What is Sushil's problem today? Who wound him up?

Who's behind all this?

If you ask this question, you are looking for either a troublemaker or someone responsible. Another way to phrase this question is "who is responsible for what happened?"

Example:

- Stop fighting you two. Now, who's behind all this?

Wiggle his way out

If a person has said something that he regrets saying, he may try "to wiggle his way out" in order to save himself from embarrassment and other "damage."

Example:

- Politicians wiggle their way out of statements they make all the time.

Wise cracks

"Wise cracks" are sarcastic remarks.

Example:

- I'm going to the Overeater's Club and I don't want to hear any wise cracks from you.

Work around the clock

In today's terminology, it would be 24/7, twenty-four hours a day, seven days a week. Many projects require this type of work to complete.

Example:

- We need to work around the clock to get this project out to the public.

Work out the bugs

This is a term that programmers are very familiar with. "Bugs" are small problems. The phrase also applies to other projects as well.

Example:

- There are few bugs in our relationship. After we work out those, it should be great.

Work out the kinks

"Kinks" are similar to "wrinkles" discussed earlier. Kinks are small problem areas, nothing major. They are "bugs" in computer software. You want a "smooth" surface.

Example:

- After we work out the kinks in the program, it should sell fast.

Works like gangbusters

We don't say this often but it would be good to know what it means. If something "works like gangbusters," it means that it is working and flowing really well. There are no problems with it.

Example:

- Hey, it's working like gangbusters. Don't mess with it.

Yes man

A "yes man" is a person who is always very supportive of his superior no matter what. It is a demeaning term because it implies that the yes man cannot think on his own.

Example:

- Don't try to tell him about the boss. He's a yes man.

You bet your bottom dollar

This phrase means "absolutely certain."

Example:

- You can bet your bottom dollar that I'll be attending her concert.

You can dress him up but you can't take him out

This is a phrase that is used to mean that a person might be an embarrassment in public. It is used jokingly.

Example:

- You can certainly dress him up but you can't take him out.

You can see right through him

This means that a person is transparent. If he is lying, you know it. If he is honest, you know it. If he is happy, you know it. If he is angry, you know it. Usually, though, it means that you know that a person is lying.

Example:

- I knew he was lying when he opened his mouth. I could see right through him.

You can take that to the bank

This means "it is a certain thing." A similar, related phrase is "you can bank on it."

Example:

- He's finally coming home for Christmas. You can take that to the bank!

You can't beat that with a stick

This means that you have found a really good bargain. Often you will hear it without the words "with a stick."

Example:

- 1000 for that stereo? You can't beat that with a stick.

You can't pull the wool over his eyes

This phrase simply means that you cannot fool or trick him. It is often used jokingly.

Example:

- Hey, he's a college graduate. You can't pull the wool over his eyes.

You have a rough life

This phrase is used when you see a person relaxing and

enjoying his position. Perhaps he is by a swimming pool when others are at work. It is said jokingly.

Example:

- You have a rough life. Are you sure we can't get you another beer or something?

You just can't find good help these days

Often it is used in jest about small mistakes an employee is making. Also, you use this phrase sarcastically just after you fire someone or let them go.

Example:

- That's the third worker I've fired in two weeks. You just can't find good help these days.

You nailed it

This is a hard phrase to define, though you will hear it often. It means to get it exactly right. You can "nail something" in sports, in a speech and with a solid idea.

Example:

- You really nailed that speech! Great job.

You need to drown him out

When you "drown something out," you are louder than that noise.

Example:

- Often, at a stoplight, the car beside me is drowning out the radio station I'm listening to.

You take my breath away

A man might say this to a woman when he sees her in a lovely dress. If he is breathless, he really doesn't know what else to say to compliment her.

Example:

- When I saw her in the mirror, she literally took my breath away.

You take the reins

This means "you are in control now. You are the boss. Tell us what to do?" Reins are the "strings" you use to control a horse when riding a horse.

Example:

- He told me to take the reins after he saw how I managed the small software project.

Your better half

"Your better half" is always your spouse, and usually it refers to the wife.

Example:

- Where's your better half today?

Commonly used Proverbs & Sayings

absence makes the heart grow fonder

- being away from someone makes you like him or her even more

Example:

- Absence makes the heart grow fonder and when the young man went away to university he missed his girlfriend even more.

actions speak louder than words

- what you do is more important than what you say

Example:

- The politician promised to do many things but he never did anything. But actions speak louder than words and he lost the next election.

all good things must come to an end

- an enjoyable experience ends

Example:

- All good things must come to an end and we soon had to return home from our holiday.

all is fair in love and war

- anything that you do in love or in war can be excused

Example:

- All is fair in love and war the man thought when he asked his colleague for a date.

all's well that ends well

- if things are good in the end then we should be satisfied (from Shakespeare's play All's Well That Ends Well)

Example:

- All's well that ends well and although the storm was very bad the children arrived home safely.

all roads lead to Rome

- the same end or goal may be reached by many different ways

Example:

- All roads lead to Rome and the two groups used two different methods to finish the project.

all that glitters is not gold

- many things that look attractive and valuable actually have no value at all

Example:

- The man learned that all that glitters is not gold when he invested his money in the stock market and lost much of it.

all work and no play makes Jack a dull boy

- it is not healthy to spend all of your time working and never relaxing or playing

Example:

- The parents always wanted their child to study and did not realise that all work and no play makes Jack a dull boy.

any port in a storm

- when someone is faced with an emergency he or she will accept help from any source and in any place - even from someone who they do not like

Example:

- There was a bad storm so the ship went to the nearest port. It was any port in a storm.

bad news travels fast

- people are quicker to pass on bad news than good news

Example:

- Bad news travels fast and the man heard about the job layoffs a week before the official announcement.

a bad workman blames his tools

- someone blames his tools or the material that he is working with for his own bad work

Example:

- The carpenter was angry that his saw did not cut well. As often happens, a bad workman blames his tools.

bark is worse than one's bite

- someone is not as bad-tempered as they appear

Example:

- The supervisor was always threatening to fire anyone who was late but he never did anything. His bark was worse than his bite.

beauty is only skin deep

- looks are superficial and sometimes a beautiful person may have unpleasant characteristics

Example:

- The woman is not beautiful but beauty is only skin deep and her personality is wonderful.

beggars can't be choosers

- one should not criticize something that one gets for free

Example:

- Beggars can't be choosers and the girl should not complain about the free furniture that she got from a friend.

better late than never

- it is better to do something late than to never do it at all

Example:

- The boy finally got a job after not working for three years but at least it was better late than never.

better safe than sorry

- it is better to be careful than to take a chance and risk an accident or illness or failure which you may regret

Example:

- It is better to be safe than sorry and I always bring my umbrella to work when it is cloudy day.

better the devil you know than the devil you don't

- it may be better to endure a situation that you are accustomed to than to risk change for something that may be worse

Example:

- My friend wanted to change banks but he felt that it was better the devil he knew than the devil he didn't so he stayed with his old bank.

between the devil and the deep blue sea

- you have two choices or alternatives and both of them are unpleasant

Example:

- We are between the devil and the deep blue sea. If we

increase our prices we won't sell our products. If we lower our prices we will lose money.

bird in hand is worth two in the bush

- do not risk losing something that you have by trying to get something that is not certain

Example:

- "You should accept the job offer with the lower salary now rather than waiting for better job. Remember that a bird in hand is worth two in the bush."

birds of a feather flock together

- people who are similar often become friends or spend time together

Example:

- The four boys were similar in every way and a good example that birds of a feather flock together.

blind leading the blind

- someone who has little ability or knowledge but is trying to help or teach someone else

Example:

- It was the blind leading the blind when the teacher who could not cook was asked to teach the cooking class.

blood is thicker than water

- family ties are stronger than other relationships

Example:

- Blood is thicker than water and the man chose to help his family rather than his friends.

boys will be boys

- you should not criticise boys or men for being adventurous or mischievous or noisy because that is how you should expect them to behave

Example:

- Boys will be boys and the two brothers always come home very dirty.

cat has nine lives

- cats are very strong and can survive many accidents or problems

Example:

- The President of the small country survived crisis after crisis just like a cat with nine lives.

charity begins at home

- one should help one's family or close friends before helping other people

Example:

- The man was always doing volunteer work. He did not understand that charity begins at home and he should spend more time helping his own family.

children and fools speak the truth

- children and fools say things without knowing or thinking what they mean but often what they say is true

Example:

- The child said that the woman was too fat which was true. Children and fools do speak the truth.

children should be seen and not heard

- children should be quiet

Example:

- The woman believed that children should be seen and not heard. And her children were always very quiet.

cleanliness is next to godliness

- being a clean person is next in importance in life to having good religious or moral values

Example:

- The mother told her children that cleanliness is next to godliness when she asked them to clean their rooms.

crime doesn't pay

- crime is not profitable or beneficial and you will probably be caught and punished if you commit a crime

Example:

- The young man learned that crime doesn't pay when he was arrested for stealing the bicycle.

curiosity killed the cat

- asking questions or being curious about something that is not your business is often not a good thing

Example:

- "Curiosity killed the cat," the mother said as the child asked questions about her birthday party.

customer is always right

- you should not disagree with your customers no matter what the problem is or you may lose your customer

Example:

- The sales clerks were trained that the customer is always right and they must never argue with a customer.

devil take the hindmost

- everybody must look after their own interests or safety

Example:

- The man's attitude was the devil take the hindmost and he never helped his friends when they needed help.

die is cast

- a decision has already been made and you cannot change it

Example:

- We have decided to move to Paris. Now the die is cast and we cannot change our plans.

different strokes for different folks

- everyone has different interests and tastes

Example:

- The man loves to read all night and sleep all day. It is definitely different strokes for different folks.

discretion is the better part of valor

- it is better to be careful and use discretion than to be too courageous and take unnecessary risks

Example:

- Discretion is the better part of valor and the man decided not to make a complaint against his company.

do as I say, not as I do

- to follow someone's advice and not their actions

Example:

- The man always said to do as he says and not as he does because his advice was always better than his actions

do as you would be done by

- treat other people the way that you would like them to treat you

Example:

- "If you do not want people to criticise you, then you should not criticise other people. Remember to do as you would be done by."

do unto others as you would have others do unto you

- treat other people the way that you would like them to treat you

Example:

- "Don't hurt the feelings of your friend. Remember, do unto others as you would have them do unto you."

early bird catches the worm

- arriving early gives one an advantage

Example:

- My boss always comes to work early because he believes that the early bird catches the worm.

early to bed, early to rise makes one healthy, wealthy and wise

- going to bed early is good for you

Example:

- Early to bed, early to rise makes one healthy, wealthy and wise was the advice that my grandmother gave me.

easier said than done

- something is easier to suggest or talk about than to actually do

Example:

- It is easier said than done to decide that you will never eat chocolate again.

easy come, easy go

- something that you easily acquire may be easily spent/ lost/wasted

Example:

- The man always found a new job easily but then he would often quit the job quickly. For him it was always easy come, easy go.

eat, drink, and be merry

- enjoy yourself while you can without thinking about the future

Example:

- The sailors always tried to eat, drink and be merry before they went on a voyage.

empty vessels make the most noise

- people who are the least intelligent are often the loudest and talk the most

Example:

- The man talked endlessly but he never knew much about what he was saying. He was a good example that empty vessels make the most noise.

every cloud has a silver lining

- there is always something good in every problem or bad event

Example:

- Although the fire destroyed the small business, every cloud has a silver lining and the business owners were able to build a new building which was better than the original one.

every dog has his day

- everyone will have his chance or turn

Example:

- My friend is very discouraged because of his recent bad luck. However, every dog has his day and he should soon overcome those problems and find success.

exception proves the rule

- something that is different from what you believe or expect can prove that the belief is often true

Example:

- All of the salespeople at the office are very talkative and outgoing but one person is the exception that proves the rule. He is very quiet and shy.

eye for an eye and a tooth for a tooth

- a crime or injury should be paid back equally

Example:

- The athlete believed in an eye for an eye and a tooth for a tooth and he attacked the player who had hurt him during the previous game.

eyes are bigger than one's stomach

- when someone takes more food than he or she can eat

Example:

- My eyes were bigger than my stomach at the buffet and I was unable to eat all of the food that I took.

a faint heart never won a lady

- a shy or timid person must be bold to attract the woman that he likes

Example:

- The man must be more aggressive if he wants to find a girlfriend. He should remember that a faint heart never won a lady.

familiarity breeds contempt

- knowing a person closely for a long time sometimes leads to bad feelings

Example:

- Familiarity breeds contempt and after living together for several months the two girls were always fighting.

fat is in the fire

- something unwise has been said or done which may cause problems or trouble

Example:

- The woman said that her colleague was stealing office materials. Now, the fat is in the fire and a serious problem may be developing.

finders keepers, losers weepers

- the person who finds something can keep it and the person who loses it can only cry because it is gone

Example:

- Finders keepers, losers weepers thought the boy when he found the beautiful pocketknife in the park.

first come, first served

- the person who comes first will have his turn first or be served something first

Example:

- It was first come, first served at the banquet so we went to the food table quickly.

first time for everything

- just because something has not been done or happened before does not mean that it will never happen

Example:

- There is a first time for everything and the man recently decided to try skydiving.

flattery will get you nowhere

- praise or flattery will not convince someone to do something that he or she does not want to do

Example:

- "Flattery will get you nowhere," the woman said to the man who was giving her compliments.

fools rush in where angels fear to tread

- inexperienced people with little knowledge often become involved in difficult situations that smarter people would avoid

Example:

- Fools rush in where angels fear to tread and when

house prices became very high many people decided to buy a house.

a friend in need is a friend indeed

- a friend who helps you when you need help is a true friend

Example:

- He was my best friend since childhood so naturally I helped him when he got into trouble. We both know that a friend in need is a friend indeed.

give a dog a bad name (and hang him)

- it is difficult to regain a reputation that has been lost

Example:

- It is easy to give a dog a bad name but now it will take a long time for the store to regain their good reputation after the scandal.

give (someone) an inch and they will take a mile

- if you give a little to someone then they will then ask for more

Example:

- The teacher was always strict in his classroom. He knew that if he gave the pupils an inch they would take a mile and he would lose all control.

give the devil his due

- to recognise the good points of someone who you think is unworthy

Example:

- We do not like the man's personality but you must give the devil his due, his workmanship is wonderful.

grass is always greener on the other side (of the fence)

- a place or a situation that is far away or different seems better than one's present situation

Example:

- My cousin is always looking for a new job. For her the grass is always greener on the other side of the fence.

half a loaf is better than none

- having part of something is better than having nothing

Example:

- Half a loaf is better than none and you should be happy to get part of the refund back rather than nothing at all.

haste makes waste

- time gained in doing something rapidly will be lost if you must do it again to correct your mistakes

Example:

- Haste makes waste I thought as the carpenter had to repair the work that had not been done correctly the first time.

he who laughs last, laughs longest

- the person who is successful in doing something last will have the most enjoyment or success

Example:

- Everybody thought that the boy would not get the job because he was too young. However, he who laughs last laughs longest and in fact he got the job easily.

he who lives by the sword dies by the sword

- people who commit violent acts will encounter violence themselves

Example:

- The young man was involved in selling illegal drugs and he was found murdered. Sadly, he who lives by the sword dies by the sword.

he who pays the piper calls the tune

- the person who pays for something should control how it is spent or used

Example:

- The oil company was paying the expenses for the theater group. However, because he who pays the piper calls the tune they wanted to help decide which plays would be performed.

honesty is the best policy

- it is always best to be honest in everything that you do

Example:

- Honesty is the best policy and when the man found the purse on the street he gave it to a policeman.

if at first you don't succeed try, try again

- if you are patient and persevere you will achieve your goal even if you do not succeed at first

Example:

- The father taught his son to be patient and keep trying. "If at first you don't succeed try, try again," he said often.

if the cap fits wear it

- if you criticise another person and you also deserve criticism then you should accept the criticism and try and change

Example:

- The girl criticised her friend for borrowing money. However, she herself always borrowed money so she should remember that if the cap fits wear it.

if the shoe fits wear it

- if something that is said describes you then it is probably meant for you

Example:

- You should not criticise someone for something that you do yourself. Remember that if the shoe fits wear it.

in for a penny, in for a pound

- after spending some money or time for something you should spend more time or money to finish the job completely

Example:

- In for a penny, in for a pound and because we had already spent so much money repairing the car we decided to continue to pay more money until it was completely finished.

it is an ill wind that blows nobody good

- no matter how bad something is you can usually gain something from it

Example:

- The economic news was very bad but it is an ill wind that blows nobody good. Many people began to get more training in order to prepare for new jobs.

it is darkest before the dawn

- the worst or more dangerous situation will occur just before a problem is resolved

Example:

- The economic situation was terrible and just as it is darkest before the dawn things became worse before they began to improve.

it never rains but it pours

- problems often appear together in large numbers or quickly one after the other

Example:

- It never rains but it pours and we have recently had many problems with our house.

it takes all kinds (to make a world)

- different people like different things

Example:

- The woman was wearing very strange clothes. It seems that it takes all kinds to make world.

jump out of the frying pan and into the fire

- to leave one dangerous or bad situation for a situation that is worse

Example:

- My friend jumped out of the frying pan and into the fire. He changed jobs and had more problems in his new job than in his old one.

just what the doctor ordered

- something that is good for someone to have or to do

Example:

- The holiday was just what the doctor ordered and the employee returned to work energetic and refreshed.

a leopard can't change his spots

- you cannot change someone's basic human nature

Example:

- The supervisor tried to have a good relationship with

his staff but a leopard can't change his spots and he still had problems with those around him.

let bygones be bygones

- to forget the problems of the past

Example:

- My aunt decided to let bygones be bygones and she finally decided to talk to my mother again.

let sleeping dogs lie

- to not make trouble if you do not need to

Example:

- "You should let sleeping dogs lie and not ask your friend for the money that he owes you."

let the dead bury their dead

- to think about the present and try not to remember and think about past events and people

Example:

- It would be better for the woman to let the dead bury their dead and stop thinking about what happened with her sister many years ago.

lightning never strikes twice (in the same place)

- the same type of misfortune does not occur twice to the same person

Example:

- Lightning never strikes twice and I do not think that our house will be flooded again.

like father, like son

- a boy is often similar to his father

Example:

- The boy always copied his father. It was very much like father, like son.

a little hard work never hurt/killed anyone

- one should expect to do hard or difficult work and not try to avoid doing it

Example:

- The mother said that a little hard work never hurt anyone and asked her son to clean the kitchen.

little pitchers have big ears

- small children often hear things that you think they won't notice or things that they are not supposed to hear

Example:

- Little pitchers have big ears and we were very surprised that the little boy understood everything that we had said.

live and let live

- to be tolerant and accept other people who may be different

Example:

- People in a large city must learn to live and let live.

live high off the hog

- to be living in prosperous circumstances

Example:

- I have been living high off the hog since I got my new job with its high salary.

lock the barn door after the horse is stolen

- to take care or try to make something safe after it is too late

Example:

- The stadium managers tried to stop people from entering the stadium. But thousands of people had already entered. They were locking the barn door after the horse was stolen.

love is blind

- being in love with someone blinds you to his or her bad points

Example:

- The girl was not very attractive to most people but love is blind and her boyfriend loved her very much.

make hay while the sun shines

- to take advantage of opportunities and good conditions while you can

Example:

- We wanted to make hay while the sun shines so we

tried to finish the outside work while the weather was good.

many hands make light work

- a job is done easily if a lot of people share in the work

Example:

- Many hands make light work and when the three men worked together they were able to quickly finish moving the furniture.

money doesn't grow on trees

- money is not easy to get but must be worked for

Example:

- The girl's father told her that money doesn't grow on trees when she asked for money to buy new clothes.

money is no object

- there is much/enough money available so it does not matter how much you spend

Example:

- Money was no object when the new stadium was built and it had the best equipment for both the fans and the players.

money is the root of all evil

- money is the main cause of most wrongdoing and problems

Example:

- The woman stole some money from her company. It seems that money is the root of all evil, and can cause many problems.

money talks

- if you have lots of money you will be treated well, money can influence people

Example:

- We learned that money talks when the rich couple got a reservation at the famous restaurant although we could not.

more haste, less speed

- if you try to do something quickly you may make mistakes and take longer to finish the task than you would normally have

Example:

- The man was in a hurry to finish work but he made many mistakes and had to repeat some things again. This proved to him that more haste equals less speed.

necessity is the mother of invention

- if you need something you will be motivated to provide it

Example:

- Necessity is the mother of invention and we fixed the door by using an old coat hanger.

never look a gift horse in the mouth

- do not complain when you receive a gift

Example:

- You should never look a gift horse in the mouth and instead accept a gift even if you do not want or need it.

no news is good news

- when you do not receive any news about something or somebody it probably means that everything is going well

Example:

- Although the woman had not heard from her son for several weeks, she believed that no news is good news and she did not worry.

no smoke without fire

- if there are rumors or signs of something then there is probably a reason for the rumors

Example:

- There is no smoke without fire and the rumors of the political scandal suggested that it was partly true.

no time like the present

- now is the best time to do something

Example:

- We are very busy but there is no time like the present so we have decided to go to the movie as we had planned.

no use crying over spilled/spilt milk

- there is no point in worrying or complaining about something that you cannot change

Example:

- There is no use crying over spilled milk and we should not worry about what happened in the past.

nothing is sacred

- important things or situations are treated with disrespect

Example:

- Nothing is sacred and there are few subjects that the media will not talk about.

nothing succeeds like success

- when you are successful you will become more confident and gain respect which will lead to even greater success

Example:

- Nothing succeeds like success and after my sister got her first promotion she began to-do better and better at her job.

nothing ventured, nothing gained

- you cannot achieve success in something unless you are prepared to take a chance and risk failure

Example:

- Nothing ventured, nothing gained the man thought as he decided to try and begin his own computer company and see if it would be successful.

old habits die hard

- it is hard to stop doing something that has become a habit even if you want to stop it

Example:

- Old habits die hard and it is very difficult for my grandfather to change some of his habits.

once bitten, twice shy

- if something goes wrong one time then you will be careful about doing the same thing again

Example:

- Once bitten, twice shy and because the woman lost much money on the stock market she did not want to invest money there again.

one good turn deserves another

- a good deed or doing a good thing should be repaid with another good deed or by doing another good thing

Example:

- One good turn deserves another and I was quick to help my friend after he made a big effort to help me.

one man's meat is another man's poison

- what is good for one person may be bad or unsuitable for another person

Example:

- One man's meat is another man's poison and while

some people like to eat something, other people may hate the same thing.

one man's trash is another man's treasure

- something that someone thinks has no value may be considered valuable by someone else

Example:

- One man's trash is another man's treasure and people were happy to find the old furniture outside the house.

out of sight, out of mind

- something that is no longer visible will be easily forgotten

Example:

- The little boy was out of sight and out of mind until his mother discovered that he had emptied all of the shampoo containers into the toilet.

pen is mightier than the sword

- writing and ideas are more powerful than the use of force

Example:

- The general believed that the pen is mightier than the sword and he tried to use words rather than force to overcome his enemies.

penny wise and pound foolish

- to be careful with small amounts of money but to waste large amounts of money on unnecessary things

Example:

- The woman was penny wise and pound foolish and would hesitate to spend money on fruits and vegetables for her family but would buy very expensive desserts.

people who live in glass houses should not throw stones

- you should not complain about other people unless you are perfect yourself

Example:

- The man always criticises his friend for gossiping about other people but people who live in glass houses should not throw stones. He always does the same thing himself.

pot calls the kettle black

- someone criticises somebody for a fault that they have themselves

Example:

- My friend always criticises me for being late but that is like the pot calling the kettle black. He himself is the one who is usually late.

practice makes perfect

- you will become better at something if you practice

Example:

- The tennis player believes that practice makes perfect and spends every evening playing tennis.

pretty is as pretty does

- you should do pleasant things if you want people to think that you are pleasant

Example:

- Pretty is as pretty does, I said to my friend and suggested that he should be more pleasant if he wants people to like him.

prevention is better than the cure

- it is better to prevent a problem or an illness in order to avoid having to cure it

Example:

- Prevention is better than the cure and you should look after your health so that you do not become sick.

pride comes before a fall

- if you have too much pride then you may soon meet a difficulty that will make you humble

Example:

- The President of the company was arrogant about his business practices. However, pride comes before a fall and he lost his position because of a business scandal.

proof of the pudding is in the eating

- the real value of something can be judged only by practical experience and not from appearance

Example:

- The company created a new website that they thought

many people would visit butte proof of the pudding is in the eating and nobody liked the website.

put one's money where one's mouth is

- to follow through with a stated intention

Example:

- The company always says that they will buy a new computer for the secretary but they should put their money where their mouth is and buy it.

the road to hell is paved with good intentions

- you may have good intentions but if you do not put them into practice you will achieve bad results

Example:

- The man wanted to be successful at his new job but the road to hell is paved with good intentions. He was always late and he was fired from the job.

a rolling stone gathers no moss

- someone who often changes jobs or where they live does not build roots/wealth/success

Example:

- The musician proves that a rolling stone gathers no moss. He moves from town to town and has lived in almost fifty different places during his lifetime.

Rome wasn't built in a day

- it takes time and hard work to complete a difficult job

Example:

- Rome was not built in a day and the Government officials realised that it was going to take many years to rebuild the old area of the city.

seeing is believing

- you must see something before you can believe that it really exists

Example:

- Seeing is believing and until we saw the Egyptian pyramids we could not imagine their beauty.

shape up or ship out

- behave properly or leave

Example:

- The employee was told to shape up or ship out because of her bad attitude.

shoe is on the other foot

- one is experiencing the same things that one caused someone else to experience

Example:

- The supervisor treated the employees badly but now the shoe is on the other foot and his new boss treats him badly.

silence gives consent

- saying nothing or not saying no to something means that you agree

Example:

- Silence gives consent and when nobody spoke at the meeting, the principal thought that everybody agreed with his proposal.

silence is golden

- sometimes it is better to say nothing

Example:

- The man believes that silence is golden and he is very careful what he says.

slow and steady wins the race

- being patient and determined will lead you to success

Example:

- Slow and steady wins the race and the man was successful because of his hard work and patient determination.

some people are more equal than others

- the members of a group may appear equal but some members may receive better treatment than others

Example:

- Some people are more equal than others and the superstar was not given a penalty for hitting the other player while other players would have received a penalty.

spare the rod and spoil the child

- sometimes you must physically punish a child in order to teach him or her to behave properly

Example:

- The parents supported some physical punishment for their children and believed that if you spare the rod you will spoil the child.

speak of the devil (and he appears)

- a person appears just when you are talking about him or her

Example:

- We were in the coffee shop talking about our friend when speak of the devil, our friend suddenly appeared.

the spirit is willing but the flesh is weak

- someone has good intentions but their laziness or love of pleasure may prevent them from doing what they want

Example:

- The man often goes to expensive restaurants and nightclubs and although he wants to-do well at his job he cannot. For him the spirit is willing but the flesh is weak.

still waters run deep

- a quiet person may have much knowledge or deep feelings

Example:

- The salesman was very quiet but still waters run deep and away from work he was the most knowledgeable and emotional person that you could meet.

streets are paved with gold

- a place (usually a city) where you can make much money

Example:

- Many people believed that the streets were paved with gold when they moved to the city to try to have a better life.

strike while the iron is hot

- to take action quickly and at a good opportunity

Example:

- When I heard about the new job I quickly sent in my application in order to strike while the iron was hot?

tall oaks from little acorns grow

- everything has a small beginning before becoming big

Example:

- The large chain of supermarkets began with one small country store but tall oaks from little acorns grow and it was now the largest supermarket chain in the world.

tell the truth and shame the devil

- it is better to tell the truth even though there may be good reasons not tote woman had information about the illegal activities at her company.

Example:

- She was hesitant to become involved but she felt that it was better to tell the truth and shame the devil than to remain silent.

there are none so blind/deaf as those who will not see/hear

- people will not see or hear what they do not want to see or hear

Example:

- There's none so blind as those who will not see and the mother refused to believe that her son was the cause of so much trouble in the community.

there are plenty of other fish in the sea

- there are many potential partners in the world

Example:

- There are plenty of other fish in the sea, I told my friend when she separated from her boyfriend.

there is more than one way to skin a cat

- there is more than one way to do something

Example:

- When my father taught me a different way to fix the car I realized that there was more than one way to skin a cat?

there is no accounting for taste

- it is difficult to understand why another person likes something

Example:

- There is no accounting for taste I thought as I looked at the man in the red pants and the green shoes.

these things are sent to try us

- some difficulties appear in order to test our courage or patience

Example:

- The woman had very strong religious beliefs and although she faced many difficulties, she believed that those things were sent to try her and she continued on.

third time lucky

- the third time that you try something you will be successful

Example:

- The man was third time lucky when he applied for the job at the film company and he finally got the job.

the thought that counts

- the good intentions behind an action or a gift are more important than the action or the gift itself

Example:

- Although the present that the man bought for his wife was not very expensive, it was the thought that counts and his wife was very happy.

time and a place for everything

- there are times and places when something should be done and other times in which they should not be done

Example:

- There is a time and a place for everything and a symphony concert is not the place to discuss business.

time and tide wait for no man

- things will happen naturally no matter what you do so it is important to take an opportunity when it appears

Example:

- Time and tide wait for no man and if you want to become an elected official then you should take the opportunity now as it may not come again.

time flies

- time seems to pass very quickly

Example:

- Time flies and before we had a chance to enjoy the summer weather it was already autumn.

time is a great healer

- pain or sorrow will be less strongly felt as time passes

Example:

- Time is a great healer and the parents could only hope that this was true as they tried to deal with the death of their only daughter.

time is money

- time is valuable and wasting time is like wasting money

Example:

- "Time is money," the angry customer said as he waited for a long time at the car rental counter.

times change

- the values and fashions of life change

Example:

- Times change and when my friend went to buy some tapes for her tape recorder she found that they were no longer being produced.

to the victor belong/go the spoils

- the winner of something achieves power over people and property

Example:

- In ancient times a victory by an army usually meant that to the victor belong the spoils.

tomorrow is another day

- there will be another opportunity to do something in the future

Example:

- The boy gave up his plans to get on the basketball team but tomorrow is another day and he will try again next year.

too many cooks spoil the broth

- if too many people try to do something then often the job will not be done well

Example:

- There were four people trying to fix the broken air conditioner but too many cooks spoil the broth and there were too many people to do a good job.

truth is stranger than fiction

- real life is sometimes stranger than fiction

Example:

- Truth is stranger than fiction and the man survived in the mountains for several months after his airplane crashed.

truth will out

- you cannot hide the truth about something

Example:

- The politicians discovered that "the truth will out" applied to them more than to others when the media tried to learn the facts behind the scandal.

two heads are better than one

- two people working together can achieve better results than one person working alone

Example:

- Two heads are better than one and when the two carpenters began to work together they quickly solved the problem of building the cabinets.

two's company, three's a crowd

- two people (often two people on a date) are happier when nobody else is around

Example:

- The couple decided to go on a holiday with their friend but two's company and three's crowd and none of the group were able to enjoy themselves.

two wrongs don't make a right

- you cannot justify doing something wrong or bad just because somebody else has done the same thing to you

Example:

- Two wrongs don't make a right and just because the boy's friend was not punished for taking the equipment without permission, this did not make it right for others to do the same thing.

variety is the spice of life

- life is made more interesting by doing new or different things

Example:

- The three women believe that variety is the spice of life and they are always traveling to new places and trying new things.

walls have ears

- be careful what you say because someone may be listening

Example:

- We were told that walls have ears when our supervisor heard us talking in the hall.

waste not, want not

- if you never waste anything then you will not lack for anything either

Example:

- The children were very poor when they were young and were taught by their parents to waste not, want not.

watched pot never boils

- if you wait impatiently for something to happen then it will seem to take longer

Example:

- "You should go and sit down rather than wait for the beans to cook. Remember that a watched pot never boils."

the way to a man's heart is through his stomach

- a woman can win a man's love if she gives him the food that he likes

Example:

- The woman believed that the way to a man's heart is through his stomach and she spent a lot of time cooking for her husband.

what goes around comes around

- justice will be served and you will get what you deserve

Example:

- What goes around comes around and it is wise to maintain good relations with the people who you work with.

what the eye doesn't see the heart doesn't grieve over

- you will not be troubled by something you do not know exists

Example:

- "Ignore the new furniture that your neighbors recently purchased. Remember that what the eye doesn't see the heart doesn't grieve over."

when in Rome do as the Romans do

- you should adjust your habits to match the customs of the people or place where you live

Example:

- The diplomat believed that when in Rome do as the Romans do and he made an effort to learn the language and the customs of the people where he lived and worked.

when it rains it pours

- problems often appear together in large numbers or quickly one after the other

Example:

- When it rains it pours and much time was spent dealing with problem after problem caused by the new accounting system?

when pigs fly

- something is impossible (used when you do not believe something will happen)

Example:

- I think that my friend will finish his university degree when pigs fly. Probably never.

when the cat's away the mice will play

- when someone in charge of children/students/workers is away then they will enjoy themselves and stop working

Example:

- The teacher returned to the classroom and everyone was running around. It was a perfect example that when the cat's away the mice will play.

where there's a will there's a way

- if you are sufficiently determined you can overcome difficulties and do what you want to do

Example:

- Where there's a will there's a way and the young woman worked very hard to get enough money to go to the computer school?

where there's smoke there's fire

- if there is evidence of a problem then there probably is a problem

Example:

- Where there's smoke there's fire and the discussion of the safety problem suggested that the company should try to do something about it?

the wish is father to the thought

- you want something to be true so you begin to think that it is true

Example:

- The wish is father to the thought and the woman believed that her boyfriend wanted to get married even though he did not.

you are only young once

- enjoy life while you are young and before you must face the responsibilities of life

Example:

- The young man's grandmother believed that you are only young once and encouraged her grandson to do many new things in his life.

you are what you eat

- in order to be fit and healthy you need to eat good food

Example:

- You are what you eat so you should try to eat healthy food.

you can lead/take a horse to water but you can't make him drink

- you can give someone the opportunity to do something but you can't get him or her to do it if they don't want to

Example:

- The woman took her children to the park but they were not interested in playing in the playground. You can lead a horse to water but you can't make him drink.

you can't teach an old dog new tricks

- people become used to their way of doing things and you can't get them to change

Example:

- My friend refused to try anything new and would never go to a new restaurant. It is true that you can't teach old dog new tricks.

you make your bed and you must lie on it

- you will suffer the results of your own actions, you are responsible for your actions

Example:

- The man refused to wear his rubber boots when he went out in the rain. Now he must spend the day wearing wet clothes. He made his bed and now he must lie on it.

7

Phrasal Verbs

1. **ask someone out**

Meaning: invite on a date

- Brian asked Judy out to dinner and a movie.

2. **ask around**

Meaning: ask many people the same question

- I asked around but nobody has seen my wallet.

3. **add up to something**

Meaning: equal

- Your purchases add up to 5000 rupees.

4. **back something up**

Meaning: reverse

- You'll have to back up your car so that I can get out.

5. **back someone up**

Meaning: support

- My wife backed me up over my decision to quit my job.

6. blow up

Meaning: explode

- The racing car blew up after it crashed into the fence.

7. blow something up

Meaning: add air

- We have to blow 50 balloons up for the party.

8. break down

Meaning: stop functioning (vehicle, machine)

- Our car broke down at the side of the highway in the snowstorm.

9. break down

Meaning: get upset

- The woman broke down when the police told her that her son had died.

10. break something down

Meaning: divide into smaller parts

- Our teacher broke the final project down into three separate parts.

11. break in

Meaning: force entry to a building

- Somebody broke in last night and stole our stereo.

12. break into something

Meaning: enter forcibly

- The firemen had to break into the room to rescue the children.

13. break something in

Meaning: wear something a few times so that it doesn't look/feel new

- I need to break these shoes in before we run next week.

14. break in

Meaning: interrupt

- The TV station broke in to report the news of the president's death.

15. break up

Meaning: end a relationship

- My boyfriend and I broke up before I moved to America.

16. break up

Meaning: start laughing (informal)

- The kids just broke up as soon as the clown started talking.

17. break out

Meaning: escape

- The prisoners broke out of jail when the guards weren't looking.

18. break out in something

Meaning: develop a skin condition

- I broke out in a rash after our camping trip.

19. bring someone down

Meaning: make unhappy

- This sad music is bringing me down.

20. bring someone up

Meaning: raise a child

- My grandparents brought me up after my parents died.

21. bring something up 1

Meaning: start talking about a subject

- My mother walks out of the room when my father brings up sports.

22. bring something up 2

Meaning: vomit

- He drank so much that he brought his dinner up in the toilet.

23. call around

Meaning: phone many different places/people

- We called around but we weren't able to find the car part we needed.

24. call someone back

Meaning: return a phone call

- I called the company back but the offices were closed for the weekend.

25. call something off

Meaning: cancel

- Jatin called the wedding off because he wasn't in love with his fiancé.

26. call on someone

Meaning: ask for an answer or opinion

- The professor called on me for question 1.

27. call on someone

Meaning: visit someone

- We called on you last night but you weren't home.

28. call someone up

Meaning: phone

- Give me your phone number and I will call you up when we are in town.

29. calm down

Meaning: relax after being angry

- You are still mad. You need to calm down before you drive the car.

30. not care for someone/something

Meaning: **not like (formal)**

- I don't care for his behaviour.

31 catch up

Meaning: **get to the same point as someone else**

- You'll have to run faster than that if you want to catch up with Marty.

32. check in

Meaning: **arrive and register at a hotel or airport**

- We will get the hotel keys when we check in.

33. check out

Meaning: leave a hotel

- You have to check out of the hotel before 11:00 AM.

34. check someonesomething out

Meaning: **ok at carefully, investigate**

- The company checks out all new employees.

35. check out someone/something

Meaning: look at (informal)

- Check out the crazy hair on that guy!

36. cheer up

Meaning: become happier

- She cheered up when she heard the good news.

37. cheer someone up

Meaning: make happier

- I brought you some flowers to cheer you up.

38. clean something up

Meaning: tidy, clean

- Please clean up your bedroom before you go outside.

39. come across something

Meaning: find unexpectedly

- I came across these old photos when I was tidying the closet.

40. come apart

Meaning: separate

- The top and bottom come apart if you pull hard enough.

41. come down with something

Meaning: become sick

- My nephew came down with chicken pox this weekend.

42. come forward

Meaning: volunteer for a task or to give evidence

- The woman came forward with her husband's finger prints.

43. come from somewhere

Meaning: originate in

- The art of origami comes from Asia.

44. count on someone/something

Meaning: rely on

- I am counting on you to make dinner while I am out.

45. cross something out

Meaning: draw a line through

- Please cross out your old address and write your new one.

46. cut back on something

Meaning: consume less

- My doctor wants me to cut back on sweets and fatty foods.

47. cut something down

Meaning: make something fall to the ground

- We had to cut the old tree in our yard down after the storm.

48. cut in

Meaning: interrupt

- Your father cut in while I was dancing with your uncle.

49. cut in

Meaning: pull in too closely in front of another vehicle

- The bus driver got angry when that car cut in.

50. cut in

Meaning: start operating (of an engine or electrical device)

- The air conditioner cuts in when the temperature gets to 22°C.

51. cut something off

Meaning: remove with something sharp

- The doctors cut off his leg because it was severely injured.

52. cut something off

Meaning: stop providing

- The phone company cut-off our phone because we didn't pay the bill.

53. cut someone off

Meaning: take out of a will

- My grandparents cut my father off when he remarried.

54. cut something out

Meaning: remove part of something (usually with scissors and paper)

- I cut this ad out of the newspaper.

55. do something over

Meaning: do again

- My teacher wants me to do my essay over because she doesn't like my topic.

56. do away with something

Meaning: discard

- It's time to do away with all of these old tax records.

57. do something up

Meaning: fasten, close

- Do your coat up before you go outside. It's snowing!

58. dress up

Meaning: wear nice clothing

- It's a fancy restaurant so we have to dress up.

59. drop back

Meaning: move back in a position/group

- Andrea dropped back to third place when she fell off her bike.

60. drop in/by/over

Meaning: come without an appointment

- I might drop in/by/over for tea sometime this week.

61. drop out

Meaning: quit a class, school etc.

- I dropped out of Science because it was too difficult.

62. eat out/eat at a restaurant

Meaning: not willing to cook.

- Let's eat out.

63. fall apart

Meaning: break into pieces

- My new dress fell apart in the washing machine.

64. fall down

Meaning: fall to the ground

- The picture that you hung up last night fell down this morning.

65. figure something out

Meaning: understand, find the answer

- I need to figure out how to fit the piano and the bookshelf in this room.

66. fill something in

Meaning: to write information in blanks

- Please fill in the form with your name, address, and phone number.

67. fill something out

Meaning: to write information in blanks

- The form must be filled out in capital letters.

68. fill something up

Meaning: fill to the top

- I always fill the water jug up when it is empty.

69. find out

Meaning: discover

- We don't know where he lives. How can we find out?

70. find something out

Meaning: discover

- We tried to keep the time of the party a secret, but Samantha found it out.

71. get something across/over

Meaning: communicate, make understandable

- I tried to get my point across/over to the judge but she wouldn't listen.

72. get along/on

Meaning: like each other

- I was surprised how well my new girlfriend and my sister got along/on.

73. get around

Meaning: have mobility

- My grandfather can get around fine in his new wheelchair.

74. get away

Meaning: go on a vacation

- We worked so hard this year that we had to get away for a week.

75. get away with something

Meaning: do without being noticed or punished

- Lovely always gets away with cheating in his maths tests.

76. get back

Meaning: return

- We got back from our vacation last week.

77. get something back

Meaning: receive something you had before

- Shalok finally got her Science notes back from my room-mate.

78. get back at someone

Meaning: retaliate, take revenge

- My sister got back at me for stealing her shoes. She stole my favourite hat.

79. get back into something

Meaning: become interested in something again

- I finally got back into my novel and finished it.

80. get on something

Meaning: step onto a vehicle

- We're going to freeze out here if you don't let us get on the bus.

81. get over something

Meaning: recover from an illness, loss, difficulty

- I just got over the flu and now my sister has it.

82. get over something

Meaning: overcome a problem

- The company will have to close if it can't get over the new regulations.

83. get round to something

Meaning: finally find time to do

- I don't know when I am going to get round to writing the thank you cards.

84. get together

Meaning: meet (usually for social reasons)

- Let's get together for a BBQ this weekend.

85. get up

Meaning: get out of bed

- I got up early today to study for my exam.

86. get up

Meaning: stand

- You should get up and give the elderly man your seat.

87. give someone away

Meaning: reveal hidden information about someone

- His wife gave him away to the police.

88. give someone away

Meaning: take the bride to the altar

- My father gave me away at my wedding.

89. give something away

Meaning: ruin a secret

- My little sister gave the surprise party away by accident.

90. give something back

Meaning: return a borrowed item

- I have to give these skates back to Rahul before his hockey game.

91. give in reluctantly

Meaning: stop fighting or arguing

- My boyfriend didn't want to go to the ballet, but he finally gave in.

92. give something out

Meaning: give to many people (usually at no cost)

- They were giving out free perfume samples at the department store.

93. give something up

Meaning: quit a habit

- I am giving up smoking as of January 1st.

94. give up

Meaning: stop trying

- My maths homework was too difficult so I gave up.

95. go after someone

Meaning: follow someone

- My brother tried to go after the thief in his car.

96. go after something

Meaning: try to achieve something

- I went after my dream and now I am a published writer.

97. go against someone

Meaning: compete, oppose

- We are going against the best soccer team in the city tonight.

98. go ahead

Meaning: start, proceed

- Please go ahead and eat before the food gets cold.

99. go back

Meaning: return to a place

- I have to go back home and get my lunch.

100. go over something

Meaning: review

- Please go over your answers before you submit your test.

101. go over

Meaning: visit someone nearby

- I haven't seen Tina for a long time. I think I'll go over for an hour or two.

102. grow apart

Meaning: stop being friends over time

- My best friend and I grew apart after she changed schools.

103. grow back

Meaning: regrow

- My roses grew back this summer.

104. grow up

Meaning: become an adult

- When Jack grows up he wants to be a fireman.

105. grow out of something

Meaning: get too big for

- Sushma needs a new pair of shoes because she has grown out of her old ones.

106. grow into something

Meaning: grow big enough to fit

- This bike is too big for him now, but he should grow into it by next year.

107. hand something in

Meaning: submit

- I have to hand in my essay by Friday.

108. hand something out

Meaning: to distribute to a group of people

- We will hand out the invitations at the door.

109. hand something over

Meaning: give (usually unwillingly)

- The police asked the man to hand over his wallet and his weapons.

110. hang in

Meaning: stay positive

- Hang in there. I'm sure you'll find a job very soon.

111. hang on

Meaning: wait a short time

- Hang on while I grab my coat and shoes!

112. hang out

Meaning: spend time relaxing

- Instead of going to the party we are just going to hang out at my place.

113. hang up

Meaning: end a phone call

- He didn't say goodbye before he hung up.

114. hold someone/something back

Meaning: prevent from doing/going

- I had to hold my dog back because there was a cat in the park.

115. hold something back

Meaning: hide an emotion

- Jassi held back his tears at his grandfather's funeral.

116. hold on

Meaning: wait a short time

- Please hold on while I transfer you to the Sales Department.

117. hold onto someone/something

Meaning: hold firmly using your hands or arms

- Hold onto your hat because it's very windy outside.

118. hold someone/somethingup

Meaning: rob

- A man in a black mask held the bank up this morning.

119. keep on doing something

Meaning: continue doing

- Keep on stirring until the liquid comes to a boil.

120. keep something from someone

Meaning: not tell

- We kept our relationship from our parents for two years.

121. keep someone/something out

Meaning: stop from entering

- Try to keep the wet dog out of the living room.

122. keep something up

Meaning: continue at the same rate

- If you keep those results up you will get into a great college.

123. let someone down

Meaning: fail to support or help, disappoint

- I need you to be on time. Don't let me down this time.

124. look after someone/something

Meaning: take care of

- I have to look after my sick grandmother.

125. look down on someone

Meaning: think less of, consider inferior

- Ever since we stole that chocolate bar your dad has looked down on me.

126. look for someone/something

Meaning: try to find

- I'm looking for a red dress for the wedding.

127. look forward to something

Meaning: be excited about the future

- I'm looking forward to the Christmas break.

128. look into something

Meaning: investigate

- We are going to look into the price of snowboards today.

129. look out

Meaning: be careful, vigilant, and take notice

- Look out! That car's going to hit you!

130. look out for someone/something

Meaning: be especially vigilant for

- Don't forget to look out for snakes on the hiking trail.

131. look something over

Meaning: check, examine

- Can you look over my essay for spelling mistakes?

132. look something up

Meaning: search and find information in a reference book or database

- We can look her phone number up on the Internet.

133. look up to someone

Meaning: have a lot of respect for

- My little sister has always looked up to me.

134. make something up

Meaning: invent, lie about something

- Richa made up a story about why we were late.

135. make up

Meaning: forgive each other

- We were angry last night, but we made up at breakfast.

136.. make someone up

Meaning: apply cosmetics to

- My sisters made me up for my graduation party.

137. mix something up

Meaning: confuse two or more things

I mixed up the twins' names again!

138. pass away

Meaning: die

- His uncle passed away last night after a long illness.

139. pass out

Meaning: faint

- It was so hot in the church that an elderly lady passed out.

140. pass something out

Meaning: give the same thing to many people

- The professor passed the textbooks out before class.

141. pass something up

Meaning: decline (usually something good)

- I passed up the job because I am afraid of change.

142. pay someone back

Meaning: return owed money

- Thanks for buying my ticket. I'll pay you back on Friday.

143. pay for something

Meaning: be punished for doing something bad

- That bully will pay for being mean to my little brother.

144. pick something out

Meaning: choose

- I picked out three sweaters for you to try on.

145. put something down

Meaning: put what you are holding on a surface or floor

- You can put the groceries down on the kitchen counter.

146. put someone down

Meaning: insult, make someone feel stupid

- The students put the substitute teacher down because his pants were too short.

147. put something off

Meaning: postpone

- We are putting off our trip until January because of the hurricane.

148. put something out

Meaning: extinguish

- The neighbours put the fire out before the firemen arrived.

149. put something together

Meaning: assemble

- I have to put the crib together before the baby arrives.

150. put up with someone/something

Meaning: tolerate

- I don't think I can put up with three small children in the car.

151. put something on

Meaning: put clothing/accessories on your body

- Don't forget to put on your new earrings for the party.

152. run into someone/something

Meaning: meet unexpectedly

- I ran into an old school-friend at the mall.

153. run over/through something

Meaning: rehearse, review

- Let's run over/through these lines one more time before the show.

154. run away

Meaning: leave unexpectedly, escape

- The child ran away from home and has been missing for three days.

155. run out

Meaning: have none left

- We ran out of shampoo so I had to wash my hair with soap.

156. send something back

Meaning: return (usually by mail)

- My letter got sent back to me because I used the wrong stamp.

157. set something up

Meaning: arrange, organise

- Our boss set a meeting up with the president of the company.

158. set someone up

Meaning: trick, trap

- The police set up the car thief by using a hidden camera.

159. shop around

Meaning: compare prices

- I want to shop around a little before I decide on these boots.

160. show off

Meaning: act extra special for people watching (usually boastfully)

- He always shows off on his skateboard.

161. sleep over

Meaning: stay somewhere for the night (informal)

- You should sleep over tonight if the weather is too bad to drive home.

162. sort something out

Meaning: organise, resolve a problem

- We need to sort the bills out before the first of the month.

163. stick to something

Meaning: continue doing something, limit yourself to one particular thing

- You will lose weight if you stick to the diet.

164. switch something on

Meaning: start the energy flow, turn on

- We heard the news as soon as we switched on the car radio.

165. take after someone

Meaning: resemble a family member

- I take after my mother. We are both impatient.

166. take something apart

Meaning: purposely break into pieces

- He took the car brakes apart and found the problem.

167. take something back

Meaning: return an item

- I have to take our new TV back because it doesn't work.

168. take off

Meaning: start to fly

- My plane takes off in five minutes.

169. take something off

Meaning: remove something (usually clothing)

- Take off your socks and shoes and come in the lake!

170. take something out

Meaning: remove from a place or thing

- Can you take the garbage out to the street for me?

171. take someone out

Meaning: pay for someone to go somewhere with you

- My grandparents took us out for dinner and a movie.

172. tear something up

Meaning: rip into pieces

- I tore up my ex-boyfriend's letters and gave them back to him.

173. think back

Meaning: remember (often + to, sometimes + on)

- When I think back on my youth, I wish I had studied harder.

174. think something

Meaning: over consider

- I'll have to think this job offer over before I make my final decision.

175. throw something away

Meaning: dispose of

- We threw our old furniture away when we won the lottery.

176. turn something down

Meaning: decrease the volume or strength (heat, light etc.)

- Please turn the TV down while the guests are here.

177. turn something down

Meaning: refuse

- I turned the job down because I don't want to move.

178. turn something off

Meaning: stop the energy flow, switch off

- Your mother wants you to turn the TV off and come for dinner.

179. turn something on

Meaning: start the energy, switch on

- It's too dark in here. Let's turn some lights on.

180. turn something up

Meaning: increase the volume or strength (heat, light etc)

- Can you turn the music up? This is my favourite song.

181. turn up appear

Meaning: suddenly

- Our cat turned up after we put posters up all over the neighbourhood.

182. try something on

Meaning: sample clothing

- I'm going to try these jeans on, but I don't think they will fit.

183. try something out

Meaning: test

- I am going to try this new brand of detergent out.

184. use something up

Meaning: finish the supply

- The kids used all of the toothpaste up so we need to buy some more.

185. wake up

Meaning: stop sleeping

- We have to wake up early for work on Monday.

186. warm someone/something up

Meaning: increase the temperature

- You can warm your feet up in front of the fireplace.

187. warm up

Meaning: prepare body for exercise

- I always warm up by doing sit-ups before I go for a run.

188. wear off

Meaning: fade away

- Most of my make-up wore off before I got to the party.

189. work out

Meaning: exercise

- I work out at the gym three times a week.

190. work out

Meaning: be successful

- Our plan worked out fine.

191. work something out

Meaning: make a calculation

- We have to work out the total cost before we buy the house.

Modal Verbs

Modal verbs, sometimes called *modals*, are auxiliary verbs (helping verbs). They express such things as possibility, probability, permission and obligation.

Modal verbs to express ability

We use the modal verbs **can, could** and **be able to** + verb infinitive to talk about ability. Here's an overview, with examples:

Modal verbs to express ability

Present	**Past**
can	**could**
We use **can** when we speak about **general ability** in the present:	We use **could** when we speak about **general ability** in the past:
*Rahul **can** swim.* *I **can** play the violin. **Can** you play?*	*Picasso **could** paint when he was two.* *I **could** swim before I **could** walk.*

The negative of **can** is **can't** (cannot):

I ***can't*** *ski and I can't skate.*

The negative of **could** is **couldn't** (could not):

I ***couldn't*** *swim until I was twelve.*

Specific situations - can

We also use **can** to speak about specific situations in the present:

I can hear you but I can't see you.
Can you hear me? - Yes, I can.

Specific situations - was able to / could

We often use **was able to** when speaking about a **specific situation:**

We fixed the car and then we were able to drive home.

However, we prefer **could** to speak about a specific situation in the past when we use these verbs: **see, hear, feel, smell, taste, remember, believe, understand, decide.**

They could smell the smoke.
I could understand her perfectly.

Questions about ability - present

How many languages ***can you*** *speak?*
Can you *name all the students of your class?*

Questions about ability - past

Could you *write before you started school?*
Could you *ride a bicycle when you were small?*

Modal verbs for expressing present probability (deduction)

Some modal verbs can be used to express probability in the present and past.

Must / can't - to express probability in the present

Structure: modal + infinitive without *to*
must be, must have, can't go, etc.

We use **must** to express that we feel sure that something is true.	*They are really good, they* ***must*** *win.* *They* ***must*** *be very rich. Look at the house.*
We use **can't** to say we are sure that something is impossible.	*She* ***can't*** *be ill. I've just seen her in the shop and she lookedfine.* *It* ***can't*** *be true. I don't believe it.*

May / might / could - to express probability in the present

Structure: modal + infinitive without *to*
may be, might do, could go, etc.

We use **may** or **could** or **might** to say that it is possible that something will happen or is happening.	*They* ***may*** *be arriving tomorrow.* *He* ***might*** *be away on holiday.* *He* ***could*** *be away on holiday.* *He* ***might*** *be offered the job.*

The negative of may is may not. The negative of might is might not. They both mean that it is possible that something will not happen or is not happening.

He might not be offered the job.

I may not pass the exam.

I might not go to the match tomorrow.

We DO NOT use could not to express probability.

I ~~could not~~ go to the match tomorrow.

Modal verbs for expressing past probability (deduction)

Must / can't / couldn't have - to express probability in the past

Structure: modal + have + past participle
must have been, can't have gone, couldn't have gone

We use **must have** to express that we feel sure that something was true.

They ***must have*** *left early.*
He ***must have*** *already gone.*

We use **can't have / couldn't have** to say that we believe something was impossible.

He ***can't have escaped*** *through this window. It is too small.*
She ***can't have said*** *that.*
She ***couldn't have said*** *that.*

May / might / could have - to express probability in the past

Structure: modal + have + past participle
may have been, could have gone, might have lost

We use **may / could / might have** to say that it was possible

He ***may have missed*** *the bus.*

that something happened in the past (but we are not 100% sure).

*The road **might have been** blocked.*

The negatives are **may not have** and **might not have**.

*He **may not have left** yet.*
*The assistant **might not have received** his message.*

Should – to express weak obligation and advice

The modal verb ***should*** expresses weaker obligation than **must** and **have to**.

Should - to express obligation

Structure: should + infinitive form of a verb:
should **be**, should **go**, should **do**, etc.

We use **should** for the present and the future.
We use **should** to give advice to someone and to say that something is a good idea.
Should is weaker than **have to** and **must**.

*You **should tell** them the truth.*
*You **shouldn't smoke**, it's bad for you.*
*I don't think you **should do** it.*

Should have – for unfulfilled past obligation

Should have - to express unfulfilled obligation in the past

Structure: should + have + past participle

We use **should have** for the past.
We use **should have** to say that

*You **should have told** them the truth.*
*You **shouldn't have gone** there - it was a*

someone didn't do something but it would have been better to do it. | *mistake. I don't think you **should have** done it.*

Modal verbs in the past

Modal verbs in the past

present	past
should be	should have been
could be	could have been
will be	would be
may be	may have been
might be	might have been
would be	would have been

Modal verbs – negatives forms

Modal verbs - negative forms

positive	negative
can (used for possibility) *It can happen; everything's possible.*	**can't / cannot** *It can't happen; it's impossible.*
can (used for permission) *Can I smoke here? - Yes, you can.*	**can't / cannot / mustn't** *You can't smoke here. You mustn't smoke here.*
can (used for ability) *I can play the guitar.*	**can't / cannot** *I can't play the guitar.*
must / have to / has to (used for obligation)	**don't have to / needn't**

You must be there at 8 o'clock.	*You don't have to be there at 8 o'clock.*
You have to be there at 8 o'clock.	*You needn't be there at 8 o'clock.*
must (used for personal opinion, certainty)	**can't**
He must be here - I can see his car.	*He can't be here - his car's not outside.*
might / may (used for personal opinion, certainty)	**may not / might not**
He might/may be late today - there's a lot of traffic on the roads.	*He might/may not get here on time - there's a lot of traffic on the roads.*
should (used for weak obligation / advice)	**shouldn't**
You should stop smoking because it's unhealthy.	*You shouldn't smoke so much - it's unhealthy. You shouldn't spend so much time watching TV.*

"Had to" vs. "must have"

The modal verb "must" has two past tense forms: "had to" and "must have". Which form we use depends on whether we want to express obligation or if we want to say how certain we are about the probability of something happening.

This table below shows us the past tense of "must" and "have to" and when to use them.

Must / have to

present	past
When expressing obligation: *I must go. / I have to go.*	When expressing obligation, the past of 'must' and 'have to' is always 'had to': *I had to go.* *They had to be there at 2 o'clock.*
When expressing a personal opinion about probability (deduction), we use 'must' to express that we feel something is true: *He must be here.* *It must be great.*	When expressing a personal opinion in the past, we use 'must have', NOT 'had to': *He must have been here.* *It must have been great.*

9

List of Irregular Verbs

V1Base Form	V2 Past Simple	V3 Past Participle
awake	awoke	awoken
be	was, were	been
beat	beat	beaten
become	became	become
begin	began	begun
bend	bent	bent
bet	bet	bet
bid	bid	bid
bite	bit	bitten
blow	blew	blown
break	broke	broken
bring	brought	brought

broadcast	broadcast	broadcast
build	built	built
burn	burned/burnt	burned/burnt
buy	bought	bought
catch	caught	caught
choose	chose	chosen
come	came	come
cost	cost	cost
cut	cut	cut
dig	dug	dug
do	did	done
draw	drew	drawn
dream	dreamed/dreamt	dreamed/dreamt
drive	drove	driven
drink	drank	drunk
eat	ate	eaten
fall	fell	fallen
feel	felt	felt
fight	fought	fought
find	found	found
fly	flew	flown
forget	forgot	forgotten
forgive	forgave	forgiven
freeze	froze	frozen

get	got	got (sometimes *gotten)*
give	gave	given
go	went	gone
grow	grew	grown
hang	hung	hung
have	had	had
hear	heard	heard
hide	hid	hidden
hit	hit	hit
hold	held	held
hurt	hurt	hurt
keep	kept	kept
know	knew	known
lay	laid	laid
lead	led	led
learn	learned/learnt	learned/learnt
leave	left	left
lend	lent	lent
let	let	let
lie	lay	lain
lose	lost	lost
make	made	made
mean	meant	meant
meet	met	met

pay	paid	paid
put	put	put
read	read	read
ride	rode	ridden
ring	rang	rung
rise	rose	risen
run	ran	run
say	said	said
see	saw	seen
sell	sold	sold
send	sent	sent
show	showed	showed/shown
shut	shut	shut
sing	sang	sung
sit	sat	sat
sleep	slept	slept
speak	spoke	spoken
spend	spent	spent
stand	stood	stood
swim	swam	swum
take	took	taken
teach	taught	taught
tear	tore	torn
tell	told	told

think	thought	thought
throw	threw	thrown
understand	understood	understood
wake	woke	woken
wear	wore	worn
win	won	won
write	wrote	written

10

Useful Idioms

1. all of a sudden – suddenly
2. all the same - no difference
3. as a rule - usually, generally
4. as for - in reference to
5. at all - (not) in the smallest degree
6. at this point - at this time
7. be about to do something - be close to doing
8. be broke - have no money at all
9. be in charge of something - be responsible for something
10. be in good health - be healthy
11. be in poor health - not healthy
12. be in good shape - be physically fit
13. be in bad shape - be in bad state

14. be on one's way
15. be out of date - be outdated
16. be to blame - be responsible for a mistake, for something wrong
17. be used to something - be accustomed to something
18. by heart - by memorizing
19. by oneself (by myself, by himself, etc.) - alone; on one's own
20. by the way - incidentally
21. come true - become reality
22. do one's best - try very hard
23. every now and then - occasionally
24. every other - every second one
25. fall in love - begin to love
26. feel like doing something - want to do; be inclined to do something
27. for good - forever
28. for the time being - for now; at this time
29. from now on - since now
30. get in touch with someone - contact someone
31. get lost - lose one's way
32. get mixed up - get confused
33. get rid of something or someone - dispose of; discard
34. get to the point - speak directly about the subject; come to the point

35. give someone a hand - help someone
36. give someone a lift; give someone a ride - take someone to some place by car
37. in advance - well before
38. in fact - actually; in reality
39. in general - generally; generally speaking
40. in other words - using other words
41. in time (to do something) - early enough; before something begins
42. it's time - should do it right away
43. It's worth it. It's not worth it.
44. just in case - to be on the safe side
45. Just my luck! - Bad luck! Hard luck!
46. keep in mind - bear in mind; consider; remember
47. keep in touch - keep in contact by calling, visiting, etc.
48. keep one's word - fulfill a promise
49. let it go - forget bad experience; return to normal life
50. little by little - step by step; gradually
51. lose one's way - get lost
52. make friends - become friends
53. make fun of someone or something - laugh at; joke about
54. make sense - be logical

55. make up one's mind - decide
56. Make yourself at home. - Be comfortable; feel at home.
57. never mind - don't worry about it
58. not to mention - in addition to
59. no wonder - not surprising
60. on credit - not having to pay cash right away
61. on guard - on the alert
62. on hand - available
63. on one's own (on my own, on your own, on his own, etc.) - alone; by oneself
64. on purpose - intentionally
65. on second thought - after thinking again
66. on the alert - on guard
67. on the other hand - considering the other side of the question
68. on time - punctually; at the specified time
69. out of the question - impossible
70. pay attention - be attentive
71. right away - immediately
72. so far - up to now
73. take a break - stop for rest
74. take care of someone or something - look after; see that something is done properly
75. take into account - consider something

76. take it easy - relax; be calm
77. take part in something - participate
78. take place - happen
79. take time - take a long time
80. take turns - alternate doing something one after another
81. That's just the point. - That's it.
82. that will do - it's enough
83. under the weather - feeling a little ill, a little unwell
84. (be) up to date - modern, latest, current
85. used to do something - did something regularly in the past but not now
86. What's the matter? - What is it?
87. would rather - prefer

11

Similes-Idiomatic Comparisons

1. As alike as two peas in a pod
2. As American as apple pie
3. As bald as a coot
4. As black as Newgate's knocker
5. As black as coal
6. As black as pitch
7. As black as the Earl of Hell's waistcoat
8. As black as the ace of spades
9. As black as thunder
10. As black as your hat
11. As blind as a bat
12. As blind as a mole
13. As bold as brass

14. As boring as a wet weekend in Wigan
15. As boring as watching paint dry
16. As brave as a lion
17. As bright as a button
18. As bright as a new pin
19. As broad as it is long
20. As brown as a berry
21. As busy as a beaver
22. As busy as a bee
23. As busy as a one-armed paper hanger
24. As busy as a one-legged arse kicker
25. As camp as a row of tents
26. As cheap as dirt
27. As clean as a whistle
28. As clear as a bell
29. As clear as crystal
30. As clear as day
31. As clear as mud
32. As cold as a well digger's arse
33. As cold as a witch's tit
34. As cold as any stone
35. As cold as blue blazes
36. As cold as charity
37. As cold as ice
38. As common as muck

39. As cool as a cucumber
40. As crazy as a loon
41. As crooked as a dog's hind leg
42. As cross as two sticks
43. As cunning as a fox
44. As cute as a bug's ear
45. As cute as a button
46. As daft as a brush
47. As dark as pitch
48. As dead as a dodo
49. As dead as a doornail
50. As dead as mutton
51. As deaf as a post
52. As deaf as a stone
53. As different as chalk and cheese
54. As difficult as nailing jelly to a tree
55. As drunk as a lord
56. As drunk as a skunk
57. As dry as a bone
58. As dry as a pommy's bath towel
59. As dull as ditchwater
60. As dumb as a box of rocks
61. As easy as ABC
62. As easy as falling off a log

63. As easy as pie
64. As easy as taking candy from a baby
65. As far as the eye can see
66. As fast as greased lightening
67. As fast as his legs could carry him
68. As fine as frog's hair
69. As fit as a butcher's dog
70. As fit as a fiddle
71. As flat as a pancake
72. As free as a bird
73. As fresh as a daisy
74. As fresh as a mountain stream
75. As full as a fat lady's sock
76. As full as an Alabama tick
77. As gentle as a lamb
78. As good as gold
79. As good as it gets
80. As good as new
81. As good as your word
82. As green as grass
83. As happy as a clam
84. As happy as a dog with two tails
85. As happy as a lark
86. As happy as a pig in shit

87. As happy as a sandboy
88. As happy as Larry
89. As hard as a rock
90. As hard as iron
91. As heavy as lead
92. As helpless as a baby
93. As high as a kite
94. As honest as the day is long
95. As hot as Hades
96. As hot as blue blazes
97. As hungry as a hunter
98. As Irish as Paddy's pig
99. As keen as mustard
100. As large as life
101. As light as a feather
102. As long as a month of Sundays
103. As long as my arm
104. As loose as a goose
105. As mad as a bear with a sore head
106. As mad as a hatter
107. As mad as a March hare
108. As mad as a wet hen
109. As many chins as a Chinese phone book
110. As merry as the day is long

111. As mild as milk
112. As miserable as sin
113. As naked as a jaybird
114. As near as dammit
115. As neat as a new pin
116. As nervous as a long tailed cat in a room full of rocking chairs
117. As nervous as a whore in church
118. As nice as ninepence
119. As nutty as a fruit cake
120. As old as Methuselah
121. As old as the hills
122. As patient as Job
123. As pissed as a newt
124. As pissed as a rat
125. As plain as a pikestaff
126. As plain as day
127. As plain as the nose on your face
128. As playful as a kitten
129. As pleased as Punch
130. As poor as a church mouse
131. As pretty as a picture
132. As proud as Punch
133. As proud as a peacock

134. As pure as the driven slush
135. As pure as the driven snow
136. As queer as a chocolate orange
137. As queer as a nine bob note
138. As queer as folk
139. As quick as a flash
140. As quiet as a mouse
141. As rare as hens' teeth
142. As rare as rocking horse shit
143. As red as a beetroot
144. As regular as clockwork
145. As right as ninepence
146. As right as rain
147. As safe as houses
148. As safe as the Bank of England
149. As scarce as hen's teeth
150. As sharp as a tack
151. As sick as a dog
152. As sick as a parrot
153. As silent as the grave
154. As skinny as a rake
155. As slippery as an eel
156. As slow as molasses in January
157. As sly as a fox

158. As small as the hairs on a gnat's bollock
159. As smooth as a baby's bottom
160. As smooth as silk
161. As snug as a bug in a rug
162. As sober as a judge
163. As solid as a rock
164. As sound as a bell
165. As stiff as a poker
166. As straight as a die
167. As straight as an arrow
168. As strong as an ox
169. As stubborn as a mule
170. As sure as God made little green apples
171. As sure as eggs is eggs
172. As sweet as a nut
173. As sweet as pie
174. As thick as thieves
175. As thick as two short planks
176. As thin as a rail
177. As thin as a rake
178. As tight as Dick's hatband
179. As tight as a drum
180. As tight as a duck's arse
181. As tough as old boots

182. As true as the day is long
183. As ugly as sin
184. As useless as a chocolate fireguard
185. As useless as a chocolate teapot
186. As useless as tits on a boar
187. As warm as toast
188. As weak as gnat's piss
189. As well as can be expected
190. As white as a ghost
191. As white as a sheet
192. As white as snow
193. As wise as an owl

12

Proverbs

1. A cat may look at a king
2. A chain is only as strong as its weakest link
3. A change is as good as a rest
4. A dog is a man's best friend
5. A drowning man will clutch at a straw
6. A fish always rots from the head down
7. A fool and his money are soon parted
8. A friend in need is a friend indeed
9. A golden key can open any door
10. A good beginning makes a good ending
11. A good man is hard to find
12. A house divided against itself cannot stand
13. A house is not a home
14. A journey of a thousand miles begins with a single step

15. A leopard cannot change its spots
16. A little knowledge is a dangerous thing
17. A little learning is a dangerous thing
18. A little of what you fancy does you good
19. A man who is his own lawyer has a fool for his client
20. A miss is as good as a mile
21. A new broom sweeps clean
22. A nod's as good as a wink to a blind horse
23. A penny saved is a penny earned
24. A person is known by the company he keeps
25. A picture paints a thousand words
26. A place for everything and everything in its place
27. A poor workman always blames his tools
28. A problem shared is a problem halved
29. A prophet is not recognised in his own land
30. A rising tide lifts all boats
31. A rolling stone gathers no moss
32. A soft answer turneth away wrath
33. A stitch in time saves nine
34. A swarm in May is worth a load of hay; a swarm in June is worth a silver spoon; but a swarm in July is not worth a fly
35. A thing of beauty is a joy forever
36. A trouble shared is a trouble halved
37. A volunteer is worth twenty pressed men

38. A watched pot never boils
39. A woman's place is in the home
40. A woman's work is never done
41. A word to the wise is enough
42. Absence makes the heart grow fonder
43. Absolute power corrupts absolutely
44. Accidents will happen (in the best-regulated families).
45. Actions speak louder than words
46. Adversity makes strange bedfellows
47. After a storm comes a calm
48. All good things come to he who waits
49. All good things must come to an end
50. All is grist that comes to the mill
51. All publicity is good publicity
52. All roads lead to Rome
53. All that glisters is not gold
54. All that glitters is not gold
55. All the world loves a lover
56. All things come to those who wait
57. All things must pass
58. All work and no play makes Jack a dull boy
59. All you need is love
60. All's fair in love and war
61. All's for the best in the best of all possible worlds

62. All's well that ends well
63. A miss is as good as a mile
64. An apple a day keeps the doctor away
65. An army marches on its stomach
66. An Englishman's home is his castle
67. An ounce of prevention is worth a pound of cure
68. Another day, another dollar
69. Any port in a storm
70. April showers bring forth May flowers
71. As thick as thieves
72. As you make your bed, so you must lie upon it
73. As you sow so shall you reap
74. Ask a silly question and you'll get a silly answer
75. Ask no questions and hear no lies
76. Attack is the best form of defence
77. Bad money drives out good
78. Bad news travels fast
79. Barking dogs seldom bite
80. Beauty is in the eye of the beholder
81. Beauty is only skin deep
82. Beggars should not be choosers
83. Behind every great man there's a great woman
84. Better late than never
85. Better safe than sorry

86. Better the Devil you know than the Devil you don't
87. Better to have loved and lost than never to have loved at all
88. Better to light a candle than to curse the darkness
89. Better to remain silent and be thought a fool that to speak and remove all doubt
90. Beware of Greeks bearing gifts
91. Beware the Ides of March
92. Big fish eat little fish
93. Birds of a feather flock together
94. Blood is thicker than water
95. Boys will be boys
96. Brevity is the soul of wit
97. Business before pleasure
98. Caesar's wife must be above suspicion
99. Carpe diem (Pluck the day; Seize the day)
100. Charity begins at home
101. Cheats never prosper
102. Children should be seen and not heard
103. Cleanliness is next to godliness
104. Clothes make the man
105. Cold hands, warm heart
106. Comparisons are odious
107. Count your blessings
108. Cowards may die many times before their death

109. Crime doesn't pay
110. Cut your coat to suit your cloth
111. Dead men tell no tales
112. Devil take the hindmost
113. Discretion is the better part of valour
114. Distance lends enchantment to the view
115. Do as I say, not as I do
116. Do as you would be done by
117. Do unto others as you would have them do to you
118. Don't bite the hand that feeds you
119. Don't burn your bridges behind you
120. Don't cast your pearls before swine
121. Don't change horses in midstream
122. Don't count your chickens before they are hatched
123. Don't cross the bridge till you come to it
124. Don't cut off your nose to spite your face
125. Don't keep a dog and bark yourself
126. Don't let the bastards grind you down
127. Don't look a gift horse in the mouth
128. Don't meet troubles half-way
129. Don't put all your eggs in one basket
130. Don't put the cart before the horse
131. Don't put new wine into old bottles
132. Don't rock the boat

133. Don't spoil the ship for a ha'porth of tar
134. Don't throw pearls to swine
135. Don't teach your Grandma to suck eggs
136. Don't throw the baby out with the bathwater
137. Don't try to walk before you can crawl
138. Don't upset the apple-cart
139. Don't wash your dirty linen in public
140. Doubt is the beginning not the end of wisdom
141. Early to bed and early to rise, makes a man healthy, wealthy and wise
142. East is east, and west is west
143. East, west, home's best
144. Easy come, easy go
145. Eat, drink and be merry, for tomorrow we die
146. Empty vessels make the most noise
147. Enough is as good as a feast
148. Enough is enough
149. Even a worm will turn
150. Every cloud has a silver lining
151. Every dog has its day
152. Every Jack has his Jill
153. Every little helps
154. Every man for himself, and the Devil take the hindmost
155. Every man has his price

156. Every picture tells a story
157. Every stick has two ends
158. Everyone wants to go to heaven but nobody wants to die
159. Everything comes to him who waits
160. Failing to plan is planning to fail
161. Faint heart never won fair lady
162. Fair exchange is no robbery
163. Faith will move mountains
164. Familiarity breeds contempt
165. Feed a cold and starve a fever
166. Fight fire with fire
167. Finders keepers, losers weepers
168. Fine words butter no parsnips
169. First come, first served
170. First impressions are the most lasting
171. First things first
172. Fish always stink from the head down
173. Fish and guests smell after three days
174. Flattery will get you nowhere
175. Fools rush in where angels fear to tread
176. For want of a nail the shoe was lost; for want of a shoe the horse was lost; and for want of a horse the man was lost
177. Forewarned is forearmed

178. Forgive and forget
179. Fortune favours the brave
180. From the sublime to the ridiculous is only one step
181. Genius is an infinite capacity for taking pains
182. Genius is one percent inspiration, ninety-nine percent perspiration
183. Give a dog a bad name and hang him
184. Give a man a fish and you will feed him for a day...
185. Give a man enough rope and he will hang himself
186. Give credit where credit is due
187. God helps those who help themselves
188. Good fences make good neighbours
189. Good talk saves the food
190. Good things come to those who wait
191. Great minds think alike
192. Half a loaf is better than no bread
193. Handsome is as handsome does
194. Hard cases make bad law
195. Hard work never did anyone any harm
196. Haste makes waste
197. He that goes a-borrowing, goes a-sorrowing
198. He who can does, he who cannot, teaches
199. He who fights and runs away, may live to fight another day
200. He who hesitates is lost

201. He who laughs last laughs longest
202. He who lives by the sword shall die by the sword
203. He who pays the piper calls the tune
204. He who sups with the Devil should have a long spoon
205. Hell hath no fury like a woman scorned
206. Hindsight is always twenty-twenty
207. History repeats itself
208. Home is where the heart is
209. Honesty is the best policy
210. Hope springs eternal
211. Horses for courses
212. If anything can go wrong, it will
213. If a job is worth doing it is worth doing well
214. If at first you don't succeed try, try and try again
215. If God had meant us to fly he'd have given us wings
216. If ifs and ands were pots and pans there'd be no work for tinkers
217. If it ain't broke, don't fix it
218. If life deals you lemons, make lemonade
219. If the cap fits, wear it
220. If the mountain won't come to Mohammed, then Mohammed must go to the mountain
221. If the shoe fits, wear it
222. If wishes were horses, beggars would ride

223. If you can't be good, be careful
224. If you can't beat em, join em
225. If you can't stand the heat get out of the kitchen
226. If you lie down with dogs, you will get up with fleas
227. If you pay peanuts, you get monkeys
228. If you want a thing done well, do it yourself
229. Ignorance is bliss
230. Imitation is the sincerest form of flattery
231. In for a penny, in for a pound
232. In the kingdom of the blind the one eyed man is king
233. In the midst of life we are in death
234. Into every life a little rain must fall
235. It ain't over till the fat lady sings
236. It goes without saying
237. It is best to be on the safe side
238. It is better to give than to receive
239. It is easy to be wise after the event
240. It never rains but it pours
241. It takes a thief to catch a thief
242. It takes all sorts to make a world
243. It takes one to know one
244. It takes two to tango
245. It's all grist to the mill
246. It's an ill wind that blows no one any good

247. It's better to give than to receive
248. It's better to have loved and lost than never to have loved at all
249. It's better to light a candle than curse the darkness
250. It's better to travel hopefully than to arrive
251. It's never too late
252. It's no use crying over spilt milk
253. It's no use locking the stable door after the horse has bolted
254. It's the early bird that catches the worm
255. It's the empty can that makes the most noise
256. It's the squeaky wheel that gets the grease
257. Jack of all trades, master of none
258. Judge not, that ye be not judged
259. Keep your chin up
260. Keep your powder dry
261. Laugh and the world laughs with you, weep and you weep alone
262. Laughter is the best medicine
263. Least said, soonest mended
264. Less is more
265. Let bygones be bygones
266. Let not the sun go down on your wrath
267. Let sleeping dogs lie
268. Let the buyer beware

269. Let the dead bury the dead
270. Let the punishment fit the crime
271. Let well alone
272. Life begins at forty
273. Life is just a bowl of cherries
274. Life is what you make it
275. Life's not all beer and skittles
276. Lightning never strikes twice in the same place
277. Like father, like son
278. Little pitchers have big ears
279. Little strokes fell great oaks
280. Little things please little minds
281. Live for today for tomorrow never comes
282. Look before you leap
283. Love is blind
284. Love makes the world go round
285. Love thy neighbour as thyself
286. Love will find a way
287. Make hay while the sun shines
288. Make love not war
289. Man does not live by bread alone
290. Manners maketh man
291. Many a little makes a mickle
292. Many a mickle makes a muckle

293. Many a true word is spoken in jest
294. Many hands make light work
295. March comes in like a lion and goes out like a lamb
296. March winds and April showers bring forth May flowers
297. Marriages are made in heaven
298. Marry in haste, repent at leisure
299. Might is right
300. Mighty oaks from little acorns grow
301. Misery loves company
302. Moderation in all things
303. Monday's child is fair of face,
304. Tuesday's child is full of grace,
305. Wednesday's child is full of woe,
306. Thursday's child has far to go,
307. Friday's child is loving and giving,
308. Saturday's child works hard for its living,
309. And a child that's born on the Sabbath day
310. Is fair and wise and good and gay.
311. Money doesn't grow on trees
312. Money is the root of all evil
313. Money isn't everything
314. Money makes the world go round
315. Money talks
316. More haste, less speed

317. Music has charms to soothe the savage breast
318. Nature abhors a vacuum
319. Necessity is the mother of invention
320. Needs must when the devil drives
321. Ne'er cast a clout till May be out
322. Never give a sucker an even break
323. Never go to bed on an argument
324. Never judge a book by its cover
325. Never let the sun go down on your anger
326. Never look a gift horse in the mouth
327. Never put off until tomorrow what you can do today
328. Never speak ill of the dead
329. Never tell tales out of school
330. Nine tailors make a man
331. No man can serve two masters
332. No man is an island
333. No names, no pack-drill
334. No news is good news
335. No one can make you feel inferior without your consent
336. No pain, no gain
337. No rest for the wicked
338. Nothing is certain but death and taxes
339. Nothing succeeds like success
340. Nothing venture, nothing gain

341. Oil and water don't mix
342. Old soldiers never die, they just fade away
343. Once a thief, always a thief
344. Once bitten, twice shy
345. One good turn deserves another
346. One half of the world does not know how the other half lives
347. One hand washes the other
348. One man's meat is another man's poison
349. One might as well be hanged for a sheep as a lamb
350. One law for the rich and another for the poor
351. One swallow does not make a summer
352. One volunteer is worth ten pressed men
353. One year's seeding makes seven years weeding
354. Only fools and horses work
355. Opportunity never knocks twice at any man's door
356. Out of sight, out of mind
357. Parsley seed goes nine times to the Devil
358. Patience is a virtue
359. Pearls of wisdom
360. Penny wise and pound foolish
361. People who live in glass houses shouldn't throw stones
362. Physician, heal thyself
363. Possession is nine points of the law
364. Power corrupts; absolute power corrupts absolutely

365. Practice makes perfect
366. Practice what you preach
367. Prevention is better than cure
368. Pride goes before a fall
369. Procrastination is the thief of time
370. Put your best foot forward
371. Rain before seven, fine before eleven
372. Red sky at night shepherd's delight; red sky in the morning, shepherd's warning
373. Revenge is a dish best served cold
374. Revenge is sweet
375. Rob Peter to pay Paul
376. Rome wasn't built in a day
377. See a pin and pick it up, all the day you'll have good luck; see a pin and let it lie, bad luck you'll have all day
378. See no evil, hear no evil, speak no evil
379. Seeing is believing
380. Seek and ye shall find
381. Set a thief to catch a thief
382. Share and share alike
383. Shrouds have no pockets
384. Silence is golden
385. Slow but sure
386. Softly, softly, catchee monkey

387. Spare the rod and spoil the child
388. Speak as you find
389. Speak softly and carry a big stick
390. Sticks and stones may break my bones, but words will never hurt me
391. Still waters run deep
392. Strike while the iron is hot
393. Stupid is as stupid does
394. Success has many fathers, while failure is an orphan
395. Take care of the pence and the pounds will take care of themselves
396. Talk is cheap
397. Talk of the Devil, and he is bound to appear
398. Tell the truth and shame the Devil
399. That which does not kill us makes us stronger
400. The age of miracles is past
401. The apple never falls far from the tree
402. The best defence is a good offence
403. The best-laid schemes of mice and men gang aft agley
404. The best things in life are free
405. The bigger they are, the harder they fall
406. The bottom line is the bottom line
407. The boy is father to the man
408. The bread always falls buttered side down

409. The child is the father of the man
410. The cobbler always wears the worst shoes
411. The course of true love never did run smooth
412. The customer is always right
413. The darkest hour is just before the dawn
414. The devil finds work for idle hands to do
415. The devil looks after his own
416. The early bird catches the worm
417. The end justifies the means
418. The exception which proves the rule
419. The female of the species is more deadly than the male
420. The fruit does not fall far from the tree
421. The good die young
422. The grass is always greener on the other side of the fence
423. The hand that rocks the cradle rules the world
424. The husband is always the last to know
425. The labourer is worthy of his hire
426. The law is an ass
427. The leopard does not change his spots
428. The longest journey starts with a single step
429. The more the merrier
430. The more things change, the more they stay the same

431. The only good Indian is a dead Indian
432. The opera ain't over till the fat lady sings
433. The pen is mightier than sword
434. The price of liberty is eternal vigilance
435. The proof of the pudding is in the eating
436. The road to hell is paved with good intentions
437. The shoemaker's son always goes barefoot
438. The squeaking wheel gets the grease
439. The truth will out
440. The way to a man's heart is through his stomach
441. There are more ways of killing a cat than choking it with cream
442. There are none so blind as those, that will not see
443. There are two sides to every question
444. There but for the grace of God, go I
445. There's a time and a place for everything
446. There's an exception to every rule
447. There's always more fish in the sea
448. There's honour among thieves
449. There's many a good tune played on an old fiddle
450. There's many a slip 'twixt cup and lip
451. There's more than one way to skin a cat
452. There's no accounting for tastes
453. There's no fool like an old fool
454. There's no place like home

455. There's no smoke without fire
456. There's no such thing as a free lunch
457. There's no such thing as bad publicity
458. There's no time like the present
459. There's none so blind as those who will not see
460. There's none so deaf as those who will not hear
461. There's nowt so queer as folk
462. There's one born every minute
463. There's safety in numbers
464. They that sow the wind, shall reap the whirlwind
465. Third time lucky
466. Those who do not learn from history are doomed to repeat it
467. Those who live in glass houses shouldn't throw stones
468. Those who sleep with dogs will rise with fleas
469. Time and tide wait for no man
470. Time flies
471. Time is a great healer
472. Time is money
473. Time will tell
474. 'tis better to have loved and lost, than never to have loved at all
475. To err is human; to forgive divine
476. To every thing there is a season
477. To the victor go the spoils

478. To travel hopefully is a better thing than to arrive
479. Tomorrow is another day
480. Tomorrow never comes
481. Too many cooks spoil the broth
482. Truth is stranger than fiction
483. Truth will out
484. Two blacks don't make a white
485. Two heads are better than one
486. Two is company, but three's a crowd
487. Two wrongs don't make a right
488. Variety is the spice of life
489. Virtue is its own reward
490. Walls have ears
491. Walnuts and pears you plant for your heirs
492. Waste not want not
493. What can't be cured must be endured
494. What goes up must come down
495. What you lose on the swings you gain on the roundabouts
496. What's sauce for the goose is sauce for the gander
497. When in Rome, do as the Romans do
498. When the cat's away the mice will play
499. When the going gets tough, the tough get going
500. When the oak is before the ash, then you will only

get a splash; when the ash is before the oak, then you may expect a soak

501. What the eye doesn't see, the heart doesn't grieve over
502. Where there's a will there's a way
503. Where there's muck there's brass
504. While there's life there's hope
505. Whom the Gods love die young
506. Why keep a dog and bark yourself?
507. Women and children first
508. Wonders will never cease
509. Work expands so as to fill the time available
510. Worrying never did anyone any good
511. You are never too old to learn
512. You are what you eat
513. You can have too much of a good thing
514. You can lead a horse to water, but you can't make it drink
515. You can't have your cake and eat it
516. You can't get blood out of a stone
517. You can't make a silk purse from a sow's ear
518. You can't make an omelette without breaking eggs
519. You can't make bricks without straw
520. You can't run with the hare and hunt with the hounds
521. You can't teach an old dog new tricks

522. You can't judge a book by its cover
523. You can't win them all
524. You catch more flies with honey than with vinegar
525. You pays your money and you takes your choice
526. Youth is wasted on the young

13

Homonyms List

- acts — things done
  ax — chopping tool
- ad — short for advertisement
  add — short for addition
- adds — performs additions
  ads — more than one advertisement
  adze — axe-like tool
- aerie — eagle's nest
  airy — breezy
- aero — of aircraft
  arrow — slender, pointed shaft
- affect — to change
  effect — result

• ail	sick
ale	beer
• all	everything
awl	pointed scriber
• allowed	permitted
aloud	spoken
• altar	raised center of worship
alter	to change
• an	a single instance
ann	a woman's name
• ant	insect
aunt	parent's sister
• ante	preliminary bet
auntie	sister of a parent
• arc	portion of a circle
ark	vessel
• ascent	the climb
assent	to agree
• ate	past tense of eat
eight	the number base of octal
• aught	anything
ought	should
• aural	of hearing
oral	of the mouth

• auricle	external part of the ear
oracle	seer
• away	distant
aweigh	just clear of the bottom
• awed	in a state of wonder
odd	not usual
• aye	naval affirmative
eye	ocular organ
I	oneself
• bail	bucket handle
bale	bundle of hay
• bailing	pumping water out of a boat
baling	wire used to tie bales
• bait	to torment
bate	to lessen
• baited	past tense of bait
bated	past tense of bate
• baiting	tormenting
bating	lessening
• bald	hairless
balled	carnal knowledge
bawled	cried aloud
• ball	playful orb
bawl	to cry

• band	a group
banned	forbidden
• bard	a poet
barred	enclosed by poles
• bare	naked
bear	wild ursine
• baron	minor royalty
barren	unable to bear children
• base	the bottom support for anything
bass	the lowest musical pitch or range
• based	supported
baste	to swab with liquid during cooking
• bases	what baseball players like to steal
basis	principal constituent of anything
basses	many four-stringed guitars
• be	to exist
bee	pollinating buzzer
• beach	where i want to be
beech	a type of tree
• bean	a legume
been	past tense of be
• beat	to hit
beet	edible red root

• beau	male friend
bow	a curve or bend; double-slipped reef knot
• beaut	slang for beauty, beautiful
butte	steep sided hill
• been	past tense of be
bin	a box or container
• beer	universally brewed comfort food
bier	a temporary frame for a coffin
• berth	anchorage
birth	your method of arrival
• besot	to get drunk
besought	past tense of beseech
• better	superior
bettor	one who bets
• bight	middle of a rope
bite	a mouthful
byte	eight bits
• billed	has a bill
build	to construct
• bit	past tense of bite
bitt	large cleat for tying up ships
• blew	past tense of blow
blue	color of California sky

• bloc	an alliance
block	square object
• boar	wild pig
Boer	a South African of Dutch descent
boor	tasteless buffoon
bore	not interesting
• board	a plank
bored	not interested
• boarder	lodger who gets meals, too
border	perimeter
• bode	an omen
bowed	curved
• bold	brave
bowled	knocked over
• bolder	more courageous
boulder	large rock
• bole	trunk
boll	round seed pod
bowl	dish
• boos	disparaging sounds from fans
booze	whiskey
• born	brought into life
borne	past participle of bear
bourn	a small stream or boundary

• borough	township
burrow	dig into the ground
• bough	tree branch
bow	front of a ship; respectful bend
• braid	a weave of three strands
brayed	a donkey cried
• braise	cook with oil and water
brays	loud, harsh cry
• brake	stopping device
break	to split apart
• breach	to break through
breech	the back part
• bread	a loaf
bred	past tense of breed
• brewed	fermented
brood	family
• brews	more than one beer
bruise	a contusion
• bridal	pertaining to brides
bridle	horse's headgear
• broach	to raise a subject
brooch	an ornament fastened to clothes
• brows	multiple foreheads
browse	grazing

• burger	meat sandwich
burgher	merchant
• bus	large multi-passenger vehicle
buss	a kiss
• bussed	kissed
bust	head and shoulders sculpture
• buy	to purchase
by	near
bye	farewell
• buyer	one who purchases
byre	a cow barn
• cache	hidden storage
cash	legal tender
• cached	hidden away
cashed	converted to legal tender
• caller	one who calls
collar	my cat has collar ID
• cannon	big gun
canon	body of law
• canter	a moderate gallop
cantor	singer
• canvas	rough cloth
canvass	to examine thoroughly

• capital	most important
capitol	center of government
• carol	Christmas song
carrel	study enclosure
• carpal	a bone of the carpus
carpel	a pistil
• cast	to throw
caste	a social class
• caster	one who throws
castor	beaver's smelly gland
• cause	generative force
caws	sounds of crows
• ceding	giving
seeding	planting
• ceiling	top of the room
sealing	to close a package or envelope
• cell	a small room
sell	to exchange for money
• cellar	under a house
seller	one who sells
• censer	incense dish
censor	bad people who fear knowledge
sensor	a device which detects

• census	numbering
senses	faculties
• cent	one hundredth of a dollar
scent	an aroma
sent	dispatched
• cereal	grains
serial	numbers in sequence
• Ceres	Roman Goddess of agriculture
series	a sequence of things
• cession	giving up
session	a group sitting
• chalk	calcareous earthy substance
chock	wedge to keep wheels from rolling
• chance	happenstance
chants	more than one litany
• chard	spinach-like vegetable
charred	burnt
• chased	quickly followed
chaste	virginal
• check	a tic mark
Czech	from Czechoslovakia
• chews	masticating
choose	to select

• choir	church singers
quire	the twentieth part of a ream of paper
• choler	yellow bile
collar	around your neck
• choral	by a chorus
coral	marine polyp skeleton
• chorale	a choir
corral	a pen for horses
• chord	three tones in harmony
cord	very light rope
cored	divested of its central part
• chute	inclined trough
shoot	to project an object
• cite	to refer to
sight	vision
site	a location
• cited	referenced
sighted	visually identified
sited	located
• cites	past tense of cite
sights	tourist rationale
sites	more than one location
• clack	a chattering sound
claque	a group hired to applaud, sycophants

• Claus	fat, jolly guy with presents
clause	contractual unit
claws	big fingernails
• clew	sheet cringle on a sail
clue	a hint
• click	ticking noise
clique	exclusive group
• climb	ascending
clime	climate
• close	to shut
clothes	garments
• coaled	supplied with coal
cold	not supplied with coal
• coarse	rough
course	path of travel
• coat	wear it for warmth
cote	small animal shed
• coddling	tenderly treating
codling	small, unripe apple
• coin	money
quoin	corner stone
• colonel	military officer
kernel	seed

- complacence — self-satisfaction
  complaisance — willingness to please
- complement — allotment
  compliment — encomium
- conch — marine mollusk
  conk — blow to the head
- coo — a soft murmuring sound
  coup — a successful stroke
- copes — gets along with adversity
  copse — a stand of trees
- cops — police officers
  copse — a small wood
- core — inner part
  corps — body
- cosign — to sign in addition
  cosine — sine of the complement
- council — group of leaders
  counsel — advisor
- creak — to squeak
  creek — small stream
- crewed — served by a crew
  crude — coarse
- crewel — embroidery yarn
  cruel — merciless

• crews	more than one crew
cruise	a sea journey
• currant	small berry
current	of the present
• curser	one who swears
cursor	on-screen positional indicator
• cygnet	a young swan
signet	an authenticating seal
• cymbal	percussive brass dish
symbol	a representation
• dam	holds back water
damn	a curse
• dammed	prevented from flowing
damned	cursed
• days	more than one day
daze	to bewilder
• dear	beloved
deer	Bambi
• dew	morning condensation
do	to perform
due	payable
• die	to become dead
dye	coloring agent

• died	passed away
dyed	colored
• dies	passing away
dyes	colors
• dine	to eat
dyne	unit of energy
• dire	desperate
dyer	one who dyes
• disc	a phonograph record
disk	a round, plate-shaped object
• discreet	confidential
discrete	individual
• discussed	talked about
disgust	sickening
• do	first note of diatonic scale
doe	a female deer
dough	uncooked bread
• doc	a physician
dock	where a boat is kept
• done	completed
dun	demand money
• dos	opposite of don'ts
dues	membership payments

• dual	two things
duel	a fight between two over honor
• earn	to come to deserve
urn	a jar
• elicit	to draw out
illicit	unlawful
• elude	to escape from
illude	to deceive
• epic	a narrative poem or story
epoch	a noteworthy period in history
• ewe	female sheep
yew	a type of tree
you	the second person
• ewes	more than one female sheep
use	to apply
yews	more than one yew tree
• eyelet	small hole for laces
islet	small island
• fain	willing
feign	pretend to be affected
• faint	pass out
feint	a weak, misdirected attack to confuse the enemy
• fair	even-handed
fare	payment

• fairing	streamlining
faring	the state of progress
• fairy	imaginary magic person
ferry	river-crossing boat
• faker	a deceiver
fakir	a Hindu ascetic
• faux	fake
foe	enemy
• fays	more than one fairy
faze	to disconcert
• faze	to stun
phase	a part of the sequence
• fazed	stunned
phased	done in sequential parts
• feat	an accomplishment
feet	look down
• ferrate	a salt containing iron and oxygen
ferret	a domesticated polecat
• feted	celebrated
fetid	stinking
• few	not many
phew	expression of relief
• file	a folder for holding papers
phial	a small glass bottle

• find	to locate
fined	to have to pay a parking ticket
• fisher	one who fishes
fissure	a crack
• flair	verve
flare	to spread
• flea	parasitic insect
flee	to run away
• flecks	many tiny specks
flex	to bend
• flew	past tense of fly
flu	short for influenza
flue	chimney pipe
• Flo	a girl's name
floe	sheet of floating ice
flow	to glide along
• flocks	more than one group of birds
phlox	a scented plant
• floes	sheets of floating ice
flows	glides along
• flour	powdered grain
flower	a bloom
• for	in place of
fore	in front

four	number after three
• forego	to precede
forgo	to abstain from
• foreword	introduction to a book
forward	the facing direction
• fort	a fortification
forte	a person's strong point
• forth	a direction
fourth	following the third
• foul	grossly offensive to the senses
fowl	domestic hen or rooster
• frees	releasing
freeze	very cold
frieze	a wall decoration
• friar	a monk
fryer	small chicken
• gaff	a barbed spear
gaffe	a mistake
• gage	a pledge or security deposit
gauge	instrument for measuring
• gait	a manner of walking or running
gate	fence door
• gaited	describing a walking horse
gated	having a gate

• gays	a frisky gathering
gaze	a languid look
• gene	a chromosome
jean	cotton twill
• gild	to coat with gold
gilled	having gills
guild	a craft society
• gilt	gold-plated
guilt	culpable
• gin	alcoholic beverage
jinn	plural of jinni, a Muslim spirit or demon
• gnawed	chewed
nod	head tilting
• gored	pierced by an animal's horns
gourd	fleshy fruit with hard skin
• gorilla	large ape
guerrilla	irregular soldier
• grade	a slope
grayed	turned gray
• graft	to attach
graphed	plotted
• grate	a lattice
great	extremely good

• grays	more than one shade of black
graze	to eat grass while wandering
• greave	leg armor
grieve	to mourn
• greaves	more than one greave
grieves	to mourn
• grill	to sear cook
grille	an iron gate or door
• groan	reaction to hearing a pun
grown	has gotten larger
• guessed	past tense of guess
guest	a visitor
• guide	one who shows the way
guyed	secured with a rope or wire
• guise	appearance
guys	Garrison Keillor's obsession
• gym	sports room
Jim	nickname for James
• hail	frozen rain
hale	robust health
• hair	grows from your head
hare	rabbit
• hairy	having much hair
Harry	a man's name

harry	to harass or hunt
• hall	a large room
haul	to carry
• halve	break in two
have	to hold in possession
• halves	more than one half
haves	those who possess
• hammock	rope bed
hummock	low, rounded hill
• hangar	garage for airplanes
hanger	from which things hang
• Harold	a man's name
herald	a horn blower
• hart	a stag
heart	blood pump
• hay	grass
hey	a shout
• hays	more than one type of hay
haze	atmospheric obscuration due to water or dust
• he'd	contraction of "he would"
heed	to pay attention
• he'll	contraction of "he will"
heal	to make well

• he'll	contraction of "he will"
hill	smaller than a mountain
• heal	to cure of disease
heel	hind part of foot
• hear	to listen
here	at this location
• heroin	narcotic
heroine	female hero
• hew	to chop
hue	a color
Hugh	a man's name
• higher	farther up
hire	to employ
• him	pronoun
hymn	religious song
• hoar	a white frost
whore	a prostitute
• hoard	a great stash
horde	a great many people
whored	prostituted
• hoarse	rough voice
horse	equine
• hoes	more than one garden weeding tool
hose	tube for watering garden weeds

• hold	to grip
holed	full of holes
• hole	round opening
whole	entirety
• holey	perforated
holy	with religious significance
wholly	completely
• hostel	inexpensive lodging for travellers
hostile	unfriendly
• hour	sixty minutes
our	possessed by us
• hours	time measurement
ours	belonging to us
• in	expressing inclusion
inn	hotel
• inc	short for incorporated
ink	writing fluid
• incite	to provoke
insight	understanding
• innocence	a state without guilt
innocents	more than one innocent
• inns	hotels
ins	those on the inside

• jam	to smash together
jamb	side post of a doorway
• jewel	precious stone
joule	unit of energy measure
• juggler	one who juggles
jugular	artery to head
• knead	working bread dough
need	must have
• knickers	woman's underwear
nickers	those who nick
• knight	chivalrous man
night	darkness
• knit	interlocking loops of yarn
nit	louse egg
• knits	verb form of knit
nits	louse eggs
• knob	handle
nob	rich person
• knock	to rap
nock	a notch in an arrow
• knot	fastening in cord
naught	nothing
not	negation

• know	to possess knowledge
no	negation
• lacks	does not have
lax	loose discipline
• lain	past tense of lay
lane	narrow road
• lam	headlong flight
lamb	baby sheep
• lay	to recline
lei	a flower necklace
• lays	to recline
laze	to recline with extreme prejudice
leis	several flower necklaces
• lea	a meadow
lee	downwind
li	about one-third of a mile in China
• leach	washing action
leech	sucking parasite
• lead	heavy metal
led	guided
• leak	accidental escape of liquid
leek	variety of onion
• lean	angle of repose
lien	a claim on property

• leas	more than one meadow
lees	the dregs
• leased	rented
least	the minimum
• lends	allows to borrow
lens	convex glass
• lessen	to reduce
lesson	a segment of learning
• liar	tells falsehoods
lyre	stringed instrument
• lichen	a fungus among us
liken	to compare
• lie	an untruth
lye	a caustic
• lightening	removing weight or darkness
lightning	static electricity from the sky
• limb	tree branch
limn	delineate
• limbs	arms or legs
limns	to illuminate, as in a manuscript
• links	pieces of chain
lynx	feral cat
• literal	taking words in their primary sense
littoral	having to do with the shore

• lo	interjection
low	not high
• load	cargo
lode	mineral vein
• load	what is carried
lowed	a cow mooed
• loan	allow to borrow
lone	by itself
• loch	a lake
lock	a security device
• lochs	more than one lake
locks	more than one security device
lox	salmon jerky
• loop	a circular pattern
loupe	a jeweler's monocular magnifier
• loos	several British toilets
lose	fail to win
• loot	ill-gotten gains
lute	stringed instrument
• lumbar	lower back
lumber	dimensional wood
• made	accomplished
maid	young woman

• mail	postal delivery
male	masculine person
• main	primary
mane	back hair
• maize	corn
maze	puzzle
• mall	hallway
maul	shred
moll	gangster's girlfriend
• manner	method
manor	lord's house
• marc	coarse brandy
mark	a sign
marque	a license to privateer; a brand
• marry	to join in matrimony
merry	happy
• marshal	to gather
martial	warlike
• massed	grouped together
mast	sail pole
• Mays	several spring months
maze	a labyrinth
• me	myself
mi	musical note

• meat	animal flesh
meet	to connect
mete	a boundary
• medal	an award
meddle	to interfere
• men's	owned by males
mends	to repair
• metal	ductile element
mettle	moxie
• mewl	to whimper
mule	offspring of female horse and male donkey
• mews	stables
muse	creative inspiration
• might	possible
mite	tiny creature
• mince	chop finely
mints	aromatic candies
• mind	thinking unit
mined	looked for ore
• miner	one who digs
minor	small
• missal	hymn book
missile	projectile

• missed	not hit
mist	fog
• misses	young ladies
Mrs.	married lady
• moan	to groan
mown	the lawn is freshly cut
• moat	water around a castle
mote	a speck
• mode	condition
mowed	a lawn in a well-trimmed condition
• mood	emotional state
mooed	what the loquacious cow did
• moor	swampy coastland; to anchor
more	additional
• moose	a large elk
mousse	dessert of whipped cream and eggs
• moral	a social imperative
morel	a mushroom
• muscles	more than one muscle
mussels	more than one mussel
• mussed	made messy
must	required
• mustard	spicy yellow sauce
mustered	assembled for roll call

• naval	pertaining to ships and the sea
navel	pertaining to the belly button
• nay	no
neigh	a horse's cry
• nays	votes against
neighs	a horse vocalizes
• neap	the lowest tide
neep	a turnip
• none	not one
nun	woman of God
• oar	boat propulsion system
or	boolean deathtrap
ore	mineral-laden dirt
• oh	interjection
owe	to be indebted
• one	singularity
won	victorious
• ordinance	a decree
ordnance	artillery
• overdo	carried to excess
overdue	past time for payment
• paced	measured by footsteps
paste	thick glue

• packed	placed in a container
pact	agreement
• pail	bucket
pale	light colored
• pain	it hurts
pane	a single panel of glass
• pair	a set of two
pare	cutting down
pear	bottom-heavy fruit
• pall	to become wearisome
Paul	barefoot Beatle
pawl	locks a ratchet
• passed	approved; moved on
past	before now
• patience	being willing to wait
patients	being willing to wait
• pause	to hesitate
paws	cat transportation
• pea	round, green legume
pee	piss
• peace	what hippies want
piece	what hippies want
• peak	mountain top
peek	secret look

pique	ruffled pride
• peal	ringing sound
peel	fruit wrapping
• pealed	rang with sound
peeled	ready to eat
• pearl	round, luminescent gem from an oyster
purl	to edge with a chain of small loops
• pearl	something of value made from an irritant
• Perl	something of value made from an irritant
• pedal	foot control
peddle	to sell
• peer	an equal (a captain at sea has no peer)
pier	wharf (a captain at sea has no pier)
• per	for each
purr	endearing cat hum
• pincer	claw-like gripping action
pincher	one who pinches
pinscher	terrier
• pistil	seed-bearing organ of a flower
pistol	hand gun
• place	a location
plaice	a flounder

• plain	not fancy
plane	a surface
• plait	braid
plate	a dish
• planar	flat
planer	one who planes
• pleural	related to lungs
plural	more than one
• plum	purple fruit
plumb	straight up and down
• Pole	a person from Poland
pole	big stick
poll	a voting
• poled	a pole was used
polled	lacking horns
• pone	the dealer's opponent in two-handed card games
pony	a small horse
• poor	no money
pore	careful study; microscopic hole
pour	to flow freely
• popery	a disparaging term for Catholics
potpourri	a miscellaneous collection

• praise	to commend
prays	worships God
preys	hunts
• pray	worship God
prey	hunt
• precedence	priority
precedents	established course of action
presidents	commanders-in-chief
presence	the state of being present
presents	what Santa brings
• pries	wedging open
prize	the reward
• prince	son of the King
prints	impressions
• principal	head of school
principle	causative force
• profit	money earned
prophet	seer
• pros	multiple experts
prose	ordinary language
• quarts	several fourths-of-gallons
qartz	crystalline rock
• quince	small, round fruit
quints	multiple quintuplets

• rabbet	a groove cut in a board
rabbit	small mammal
• rack	shelf
wrack	wreckage
• racket	illegal moneymaking scheme
racquet	woven bat for tennis
• rain	precipitation
reign	sovereign rule
rein	horse's steering wheel
• raise	elevate
rays	thin beams of light
raze	to tear down completely
• rap	a sharp knock
wrap	to encase in cloth
• rapped	knocked sharply
rapt	spellbound
wrapped	encased in cloth
• ray	arrow of light
re	musical note
• read	having knowledge from reading
red	a primary color
• reads	gets the meaning by looking
reeds	more than one aquatic plant

• real	authentic
reel	armature for winding
• recede	to move backward
reseed	to plant again
• reek	smells bad
wreak	to inflict
• resisters	protesters
resistors	electrical restrictors
• rest	stop working
wrest	take away
• retch	call Ralph on the porcelain telephone
wretch	a ragamuffin
• review	a general survey or assessment
revue	a series of theatrical sketches or songs
• rheum	watery discharge of mucous
room	partitioned space
• rhyme	a verse with regular recurrence of sounds
rime	frost
• rigger	one who rigs
rigor	discipline
• right	correct
rite	ritual
• rise	to stand up
ryes	varieties of grain

• road	a broad trail
rode	past tense of ride
rowed	to propel a boat by oars
• roil	to make turbid
royal	worthy of a king or queen
• role	part to play
roll	rotate
• rood	a cross
rude	coarse
• roomer	a tenant
rumor	gossip
• root	subterranean part of a plant
route	path of travel
• rose	pretty flower
rows	linear arrangement
• rough	coarse
ruff	pleated collar
• rout	to force out
route	path of travel
• roux	cooked butter and flour
rue	regret
• rude	impolite
rued	regretted

• sachet	a small bag containing perfumed powder
sashay	to strut or flounce
• sacks	bags
sax	short for saxophone
• sail	wind powered water travel
sale	the act of selling
• sane	mentally normal
seine	fishing net
• saner	more mentally normal than others
seiner	one who fishes with a net
• saver	one who saves
savor	to relish a taste
• sawed	cut timber
sod	turf
• scene	visual location
seen	past tense of saw
• scull	rowing motion
skull	head bone
• sea	ocean
see	to look
• seam	row of stitches
seem	appears
• seams	more than one rows of stitching
seems	it appears to be

• sear	scorched
seer	a person who sees
• seek	to look for
Sikh	Hindu religious sect
• serf	slave
surf	breaking waves
• serge	strong twilled fabric
surge	forceful push
• sew	needle and thread
so	in the manner shown
sol	musical note
sow	broadcasting seeds
• sewer	one who sews
sower	one who sows
• shake	vibrate
sheik	Arab prince
• shall	is allowed
shell	aquatic exoskeleton
• she'll	contraction of "she will"
shill	a decoy
• shear	to cut or wrench
sheer	thin; abrupt turn
• shears	cuts or wrenches; scissors
sheers	abruptly turns

• sheave	pulley
shiv	knife
• shoe	footwear
shoo	"go away"
• shoes	more than one shoe
shoos	sends away
• side	lateral
sighed	breathed sorrowfully
• sighs	multiple sad and weary breaths
size	magnitude
• sign	displayed board bearing information
sine	reciprocal of the cosecant
• sink	to submerge
synch	together in time
• slay	kill
sleigh	snow carriage
• sleight	cunning skill
slight	not much
• slew	past tense of slay
slough	bog
slue	to swing around
• sloe	blackthorn berries
slow	not fast

• soar	fly
sore	hurt
• soared	to have sailed through the air
sword	long fighting blade
• solace	comfort
soulless	lacking a soul
• sole	only
soul	immortal part of a person
• some	a few
sum	result of addition
• son	male child
sun	star
• sonny	diminutive for male child
sunny	lit by the sun
• soot	black residue of burning
suit	clothes
• sordid	squalid
sorted	arranged
• spade	shovel
spayed	to sterilize a female animal
• spoor	trail of an animal
spore	single cell reproductive body
• staid	reserved
stayed	remained

• stair	a step
stare	look intently
• stake	wooden pole
steak	slice of meat
• stationary	not moving
stationery	writing paper
• steal	take unlawfully
steel	iron alloy
• stile	narrow passage
style	mode
• stoop	a small porch
stoup	a drinking cup
• straight	not crooked
strait	narrow waterway
• succor	relief
sucker	one who sucks
• suede	split leather
swayed	curved; convinced
• suite	ensemble
sweet	sugary
• tacks	small nails
tax	governmental tithe
• tail	spinal appendage
tale	story

• tare	allowance for the weight of packing materials
tear	to rip
• taught	past tense of teach
taut	stretched tight
• team	a group working together
teem	to swarm
• teaming	a fortuitous pairing
teeming	a swarming
• tear	eyeball lubricant
tier	a horizontal row
• teas	more than one herbal infusion
tease	tantalize
tees	more than one tee
• tenner	English slang for a ten pound note
tenor	tendency
• tense	nervous
tents	more than one temporary shelter
• Thai	from Thailand
tie	a draw
• their	belonging to them
there	a place
they're	contraction of "they are"
• threw	to propel by hand
through	from end to end

• throe	a spasm of pain
throw	to discharge through the air
• throes	spasms of pain
throws	discharging through the air
• throne	the royal seat
thrown	was hurled
• tic	twitch
tick	small noise; parasitic bug
• ticks	the sounds of a clock
tics	more than one twitch
• tighten	to make tighter
titan	a giant
• timber	wood for building
timbre	musical quality
• to	toward
too	also
two	a couple
• toad	frog
toed	having toes
towed	pulled ahead
• tocsin	an alarm
toxin	a poison
• toe	forepart of the foot
tow	to pull ahead

- told — what was spoken
  tolled — a bell was rung
- tort — a sweet cake for lawyers
  torte — a sweet cake for kids
- tough — difficult
  tuff — a stratified, porous rock
- tracked — having tracks
  tract — a plot of land
- tray — a platter
  trey — three; Bill Gates' nickname
- trooper — a private soldier
  trouper — a staunch colleague
- troopers — several soldiers
  troupers — multiple actors
- trussed — tied up
  trust — faith
- vain — worthless
  vane — flat piece moving with the air
  vein — blood vessel
- vale — valley
  veil — gauzy fabric
- vary — to change
  very — extremely

• verses	paragraphs
versus	against
• vial	narrow glass container
vile	despicable
viol	stringed instrument
• vice	bad habit
vise	bench-mounted clamp
• wax	candle stuff
whacks	several blows
• wade	walk in shallow water
weighed	weight was measured
• wail	a cry
wale	welt; corduroy ridge
whale	large oceanic mammal
• waist	between ribs and hips
waste	make ill use of
• wait	remain in readiness
weight	an amount of heaviness
• waive	give up rights
wave	undulating motion
• waiver	contract for giving up rights
waver	rocking motion
• walk	perambulate
wok	Chinese cooking pan

• walks	moves by foot
woks	salient feature of a Chinese kitchen
• want	desire
wont	accustomed
• war	large scale armed conflict
wore	past tense of wear
• ware	merchandise
wear	attire
where	a place
• warn	to advise of a hazard
worn	displaying evidence of use
• warrantee	one who is protected by a guarantee
warranty	a guarantee
• warship	naval implement of destruction
worship	revere in a religious manner
• way	path or direction
weigh	to measure weight
whey	watery part of milk
• we	us
wee	very small
• weak	not strong
week	seven days
• weald	a rural area
wheeled	having wheels

wield	to apply or use
• weld	to join metal by melting its edges
welled	pouring forth
• wet	watery
whet	prime
• whine	annoying cry
wine	fermented grape juice
• whined	past tense of whine
wind	what you do to a clockwork
wined	drank well of spirits
• whirred	made a whizzing or buzzing sound
word	a speech sound
• whit	insignificant amount
wit	cleverness; sense of humor
• whither	to which place, point, condition, etc.?
wither	shrivel up
• wood	what trees are made of
would	will do
• yack	informal talk
yak	long-haired Tibetan ox
• yoke	oxen harness
yolk	yellow egg center
• yokes	more than one harness
yolks	an omelet

14

Exercises

Exercise - 1

Tick (✓) the correct answer:

1. If it's ___________ to you, let's meet on Tuesday instead of Monday.

   all along

   all at once

   all of a sudden

   all the same

2. The accident ___________ on Maple Street.

   took part

   took place

   took time

   took turns

3. Children, your task for tomorrow is to learn this poem ____________ .

   by all means

   by chance

   by heart

   by the way

4. Good-by and don't forget to ____________ !

   keep good time

   keep in mind

   keep in touch

   keep moving

5. The party was formal and dull until Mike arrived and ____________ with his jokes. Then everyone began to relax.

   broke the bank

   broke the ice

   broke the law

   broke the news

6. Mr. Milton is ____________ the Sales Department.

   in case of

   in charge of

   in honor of

   in search of

7. Will he ever come back? – No, he left ____________ .

   by himself

for good

in advance

on time

8. The car almost hit an old woman crossing the street. That was a ____________ .

   close call

   false alarm

   last-minute notice

   long shot

9. He is ____________ and will be here in ten minutes.

   about to have dinner

   behind bars

   on his way

   out of town

10. When his children broke a vase yesterday, he ____________ and began to shout at everyone?

    lost all hope

    lost his breath

    lost his temper

    lost his way

Answers:

Exercise - 1

1. all the same
2. took place

3. by heart
4. keep in touch
5. broke the ice
6. in charge of
7. for good
8. close call
9. on his way
10. lost his temper

Exercise - 2

Tick (✓) the correct answer:

1. He is all ____________ and can't install or repair anything in the house.

   elbows

   knees

   thumbs

   toes

2. She decided to try her ____________ at gardening.

   body

   hand

   head

   leg

3. She didn't have the ____________ to tell him the bad news.

   heart

   mouth

soul

tongue

4. He wanted to tell them the truth, but he got cold ___________ at the last moment.

feet

hands

knees

toes

5. He visits fashionable places where he can rub ___________ with celebrities.

arms

elbows

fingers

hands

6. Her little son is the apple of her ___________ .

eye

heart

mind

soul

7. I tried to keep a straight ___________ when she told me about her magical powers.

face

head

neck

shoulder

8. Success and money went to his ____________, and he forgot old friends.

   brain

   head

   heart

   mind

9. He wasn't able to put his ____________ on it right away, but he promised to look into the problem later.

   eye

   finger

   hand

   nose

10. I feel it in my ____________ that we are going to have problems.

    bones

    heart

    knees

    stomach

Answers:

Exercise - 2

1. thumbs
2. hand
3. heart
4. feet

5. elbows
6. eye
7. face
8. head
9. finger
10. bones

Exercise - 3

Find the most appropriate answers to these idiomatic English riddles.

1. What can you catch but not throw? – A __________ .

   ball

   bird

   bouquet

   cold

2. What has a face and two hands but no arms? – A __________ .

   clock

   mirror

   playing card

   radio

3. What can run but never walks, has a mouth but never talks, has a head but never weeps, has a bed but never sleeps? – A __________ .

   nose

   river

tree

wolf

4. What has a neck but no head? – A ____________ .

bottle

comet

flower

snake

5. What has teeth but cannot bite? – A ____________ .

bee

comb

puppy

toothpick

6. What is it that you must keep after giving it to someone? – Your ____________ .

pen

money

time

word

7. What is as light as a feather, but even the strongest man cannot hold it for much more than a minute? – ____________ .

Air

Breath

Fire

Light

8. They come out at night without being called and are lost in the day without being stolen. What are they? – ____________ .

   Cockroaches

   Nightmares

   Robbers

   Stars

9. What has been around for millions of years but is no more than a month old? – The____________ .

   moon

   sun

   universe

   wind

10. No sooner spoken than broken. What is it? – ____________ .

    Friendship

    Glass

    News

    Silence

Answers:

Exercise - 3

1. cold
2. clock
3. river
4. bottle

5. comb
6. word
7. Breath
8. Stars
9. moon
10. Silence

Exercise - 4

Complete the given crossword with the help of clues:

Across

1. As _____________ as a feather.
3. Fly like a ___________.
4. Swim like a _____________.
7. Cry like a ___________.
9. As _____________ as a bunny.
11. As _____________ as an ox.

12. As ____________ as an eel.

14. As slow as a ____________.

Down

2. As tall as a ____________.

3. As ____________ a bee.

5. As ____________ as a mule.

6. Waddle means to walk like a ____________.

7. As blind as a ____________.

8. As ____________ as a mouse.

10. As ____________ as ice.

11. As ____________ as a fox.

13. Eat like a ____________.

14. As white as ____________.

Answers:

Exercise - 4

Across

1. light
3. bird
4. fish
7. baby
9. quick
11. strong
12. slippery
14. snail

Down

2. giraffe
3. busy
5. stubborn
6. duck
7. bat
8. quiet
10. cold
11. sly
13. pig
14. snow

Exercise - 5

Fill in the blanks with 'can' / 'can't' / 'could' / 'couldn't'. If none is possible, use 'be able to' in the correct tense:

1. ________________ you swim when you were 10?
2. We ________________ get to the meeting on time yesterday because the train was delayed by one hour.
3. He ________________ arrive at the party on time, even after missing the train, so he was very pleased.
4. He's amazing, he ________________ speak 5 languages including Chinese.
5. I ________________ drive a car until I was 34, then I moved to the countryside so I had to learn.
6. I looked everywhere for my glasses but I ________________ find them anywhere.

7. I searched for your house for ages, luckily I ________________ find it in the end.
8. She's 7 years old but she ________________ read yet – her parents are getting her extra lessons.
9. I read the book three times but I ________________ understand it.
10. Karan ________________ speak Japanese when he lived in Japan, but he's forgotten most of it now.

Answers:

Exercise - 5

1. Could you swim when you were 10?
2. We couldn't get to the meeting on time yesterday because the train was delayed by one hour.
3. He was able to arrive at the party on time, even after missing the train, so he was very pleased.
4. He's amazing, he can speak 5 languages including Chinese.
5. I couldn't drive a car until I was 34, then I moved to the countryside so I had to learn.
6. I looked everywhere for my glasses but I couldn't find them anywhere.
7. I searched for your house for ages, luckily I was able to find it in the end.
8. She's 7 years old but she can't read yet – her parents are getting her extra lessons.
9. I read the book three times but I couldn't understand it.

10. Karan could speak Japanese when he lived in Japan, but he's forgotten most of it now.

Exercise - 6

Fill in the blanks with 'mustn't' or 'don't / doesn't have to':

1. We have a lot of work tomorrow. You ____________ be late.
2. You ____________ tell anyone what I just told you. It's a secret.
3. The museum is free. You ____________ pay to get in.
4. Children ____________ tell lies. It's very naughty.
5. Rahul's a millionaire. He ____________ go to work.
6. I ____________ do my washing, because my mother does it for me.
7. We ____________ rush. We've got plenty of time.
8. You ____________ smoke inside the school.
9. You can borrow my new dress but you ____________ get it dirty.
10. We ____________ miss the train, it's the last one tonight.

Answers:

Exercise - 6

1. We have a lot of work tomorrow. You mustn't be late.

2. You mustn't tell anyone what I just told you. It's a secret.
3. The museum is free. You don't have to pay to get in.
4. Children mustn't tell lies. It's very naughty.
5. Rahul's a millionaire. He doesn't have to go to work.
6. I don't have to do my washing, because my mother does it for me.
7. We don't have to rush. We've got plenty of time.
8. You mustn't smoke inside the school.
9. You can borrow my new dress but you mustn't get it dirty.
10. We mustn't miss the train, it's the last one tonight.

Exercise - 7

Fill in the blanks with 'must + infinitive' or 'must + have + past participle':

1. Kritika always does really well on exams. She ____________ (study) a lot.
2. That woman drives a very expensive car. She ____________ (have) a lot of money.
3. You ____________ (practise) a lot before you gave your speech. It was really great.
4. When Lovely got home yesterday, there were flowers on the table. Her husband ____________ (buy) them.
5. Where is my purse? I saw it earlier, so it ____________ (be) in this room.

6. Sarah couldn't find her glasses. She thought she ____________ (leave) them at her office.
7. It ____________ (be) cold outside. That man in the street is wearing a coat.
8. All my plants ____________ (be) dead! I forgot to water them before I left for my holiday.
9. Smita is so late! She ____________ (miss) the train.
10. There's rubbish all over my garden! A fox ____________ (be) in the bin.

Answers:

Exercise - 7

1. Kritika always does really well on exams. She must study a lot.
2. That woman drives a very expensive car. She must have a lot of money.
3. You must have practised a lot before you gave your speech. It was really great.
4. When Lovely got home yesterday, there were flowers on the table. Her husband must have bought them.
5. Where is my purse? I saw it earlier, so it must be in this room.
6. Sarah couldn't find her glasses. She thought she must have left them at her office.
7. It must be cold outside. That man in the street is wearing a coat.

8. All my plants must be dead! I forgot to water them before I left for my holiday.
9. Smita is so late! She must have missed the train.
10. There's rubbish all over my garden! A fox must have been in the bin.

Exercise - 8

Fill in the blanks with 'can't' or 'must':

1. Why is that man looking around like that? He ____________ be lost.
2. That woman ____________ be a doctor! She looks far too young.
3. Sonu always fails the tests, even though he's clever. He ____________ study enough.
4. The food is really good at that restaurant. They ____________ have a great chef.
5. Who's that at the door? It ____________ be Sunita she'll still be at work now.
6. This ____________ be John's house. This house has a red door, and it's number 24, just like he said.
7. Ritesha ____________ have much money, or she would buy a new car. Her old one is falling apart.
8. He ____________ be at work now, can he? It's nearly midnight.
9. What a lot of lovely flowers you have! You ____________ really like gardening.
10. Daman ____________ drink a lot of coffee. He's finished two packets already this week!

Answers:

Exercise - 8

1. Why is that man looking around like that? He must be lost.
2. That woman can't be a doctor! She looks far too young.
3. Sonu always fails the tests, even though he's clever. He can't study enough.
4. The food is really good at that restaurant. They must have a great chef.
5. Who's that at the door? It can't be Sunita – she'll still be at work now.
6. This must be John's house. This house has a red door, and it's number 24, just like he said.
7. Ritesha can't have much money, or she would buy a new car. Her old one is falling apart.
8. He can't be at work now, can he? It's nearly midnight.
9. What a lot of lovely flowers you have! You must really like gardening.
10. Daman must drink a lot of coffee. He's finished two packets already this week!

Other Books on

WORD POWER SERIES

1. Idiomatic English (How to Write & Speak It) **(New)**
2. School Essays, Letters, Applications, Paragraphs, and Stories For Higher Secondary Students **(New)**
3. Effective English Comprehention Read Fast, Understand Better! **(New)**
4. Latest Essays for College & Competitive Examinations **(New)**
5. Dictionary of New Words **(New)**
6. Art of English Conversation Speak English Fluently **(New)**
7. Teach Yourself English Grammar & Composition **(New)**
8. Common & Uncommon Proverbs **(New)**
9. Effective Editing Help Yourself in Becoming a Good Editor **(New)**
10. Effective English A Boon for Learners **(New)**
11. Essays for Primary Classes
12. Essays for Junior Classes
13. Essays for Senior Classes
14. Dictionary of Synonyms and Antonyms
15. Dictionary of Idioms and Phrases
16. Common Phrases
17. How to Write & Speak Correct English
18. Meaningful Quotes
19. Punctuation Book
20. Top School Essays
21. How to Write Business Letters with CD
22. Everyday Grammar
23. Everyday Conversation
24. Letters for All Occasions
25. School Essays & Letters for Juniors
26. Common Mistakes in English
27. The Power of Writing
28. Learn English in 21 Lessons
29. First English Dictionary
30. Boost Your Spelling Power

31. Self-Help to English Conversation
32. The Art of Effective Communication
33. A Book of Proverbs & Quotations
34. Word Power Made Easy
35. English Grammar Easier Way
36. General English for Competitive Examinations
37. Spoken English
38. School Essays, Letters Writing and Phrases
39. How to Write & Speak Better English
40. Quote Unquote (A Handbook of Famous Quotations)
41. Improve Your Vocabulary
42. Common Errors in English
43. The Art of Effective Letter Writing
44. Synonyms & Antonyms
45. Idioms
46. Business Letters